Secrets. They keep us stuck! Wherever there is a secret there is also oppression. But when God reveals truth, and a secret is exposed in a healthy manner, the enemy's power is chained, and freedom can be unleashed. I am so proud of Dennis and his family for being willing to share a few secrets, that we might be challenged to face our own. If you are struggling with something in your past, I know you will be encouraged by *No More Secrets*.

Donna Gibbs, *Author, Professional Christian Counselor,*
Director of A Clear Word Counseling Center

This book is engaging, inspirational and truth. I have said often, "what we drag out of the dark into the light, has no more power over us." Jesus said, "you will know the truth and the truth will set you free." But pouring the truth out into the open is one of the hardest things to do in life. I am proud of Dennis. He has been my friend for over a decade and his willingness to be open and vulnerable in this book is life changing.

Chonda Pierce, *Comedian*

NO MORE
SECRETS

Swanberg Ministries
2485 Tower Drive, Ste 8 Monroe, LA 71201

The quoted ideas expressed in this book (but not Scripture verses) are not, in all cases, exact quotations, as some have been edited for clarity and brevity. In all cases, the author has attempted to maintain the speaker's original intent. In some cases, quoted material for this book was obtained from secondary sources, primarily print media. While every effort was made to ensure the accuracy of these sources, the accuracy cannot be guaranteed.

. Scripture quotations are taken from:

The Holy Bible, King James Version

The Holy Bible, New International Version (NIV) Copyright © 1973, 1978, 1984, by International Bible Society. Used by permission of Zondervan Publishing House. All rights reserved.

The Holy Bible, New King James Version (NKJV) Copyright © 1982 by Thomas Nelson, Inc. Used by permission.

The Holy Bible. The New American Standard Bible®, (NASB) Copyright © 1960, 1962, 1963, 1968, 1971, 1972, 1973, 1975, 1977, 1995 by The Lockman Foundation. Used by permission.

Holy Bible, New Living Translation, (NLT) Copyright © 1996. Used by permission of Tyndale House Publishers, Inc., Wheaton Illinois 60189. All rights reserved.

The Message (MSG)- This edition issued by contractual arrangement with NavPress, a division of The Navigatiors, U.S.A. Originally published by NavPress in English as THE MESSAGE: The Bible in Contemporary Language copyright 2002-2003 by Eugene Peterson. All rights reserved.

New Century Version®. (NCV) Copyright © 1987, 1988, 1991 by Word Publishing, a division of Thomas Nelson, Inc. All rights reserved. Used by permission.

The Holman Christian Standard Bible™ (Holman CSB) Copyright © 1999, 2000, 2001 by Holman Bible Publishers. Used by permission.

Cover Design by Kim Russell | Wahoo Designs
Page Layout by Jeff Jansen | AestheticSoup.net

ISBN 978-0-692-93594-1

Cover Design by Kim Russell | Wahoo Designs
Page Layout by Jeff Jansen | AestheticSoup.net

Printed in the United States of America
1 2 3 4 5—CHG—21 20 19 18 17

NO MORE SECRETS

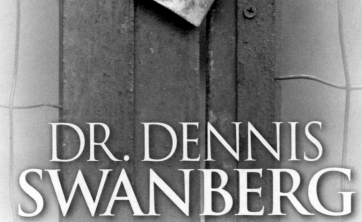

DR. DENNIS SWANBERG

Lauree and I gladly dedicate this book to
Paul and Stacy Spence...
gracious, genuine and generous servants.
We thank God for their friendship
and support through the years.

TABLE OF CONTENTS

To my sons, Chad and Dustin.
Thank you for teaching me about
'Recovery and Restoration'.
I cherish our talks on the golf course.

To my wife Lauree, my 'HoneyLove' since 1979.
Thank you for making me come off the golf course
to write this book. I knew that if I didn't finish it soon,
you were going to hide my clubs.

FOREWORD

"You need this book... it's time to get beyond the past, the pain and the secrets."

Like Adam and Eve in the garden, we all try to hide our shame, our guilt, our remorse, our pain, and our sin. Do you or someone you know or love keep secrets about your past? Have you experienced the heartache of abandonment, addiction, abortion, adultery, betrayal, divorce, poor choices, bad behaviors, inappropriate thoughts and kept silent about their effect on your life? Like Adam and Eve, have you been ashamed and thus, tried to hide your sin? I believe that covers all of us! So, YOU NEED THIS BOOK...it's time to get beyond the past, the pain, and the secrets.

Each of us are as sick as the secrets that we keep. Our sickness silently begs and pleads for healing in the secluded corners that we curl up in. Secrets are the things we hide in the dark and never bring into the light. They keep us in fear, torture, and derail us! But most devastating, they alienate us from God and keep us from his purpose in our lives. Holding on to secrets is like holding a beach ball under water. It takes work and requires that we redirect our efforts away from what we should be using our abilities for.

"America's Minister of Encouragement," affectionately referred to as "The Swan," lives a life on stage and in the public eye that seems to have no such issues, but Dennis Swanberg comes clean with us in this book. Through the experiences and circumstances that life has given him, and with permission of his family, he shares the heartache and the effect of secrets. I promise that after reading this book you will never look at Dennis Swanberg, or yourself, in the same light again.

Accurately, Dennis Swanberg believes that the sin we attempt to cover; God will uncover. Conversely, sin that is uncovered God covers with his Mercy and Grace. It is by this way of life, grounded in the radiant Truth of God, that redeems the ugly truth about ourselves, that we can be free. With no more secrets, we can find freedom in Christ and in this world.

Wrapped in the humor, love, transparency, authenticity, and grace that Dennis has been blessed with, he shares the hope and freedom that he has found and that we can have in Christ Jesus! Healing is not easy…it takes work….it involves wisdom, confession, humility, and pain…but the results are forgiveness, freedom and restoration!

God has been using Dennis to help the hurting for decades and I cannot wait to see how God is going to use this book! May we all live in the light of Truth…Freedom and…With No More Secrets.

Tim Clinton, *President*
American Association of Christian Counselors

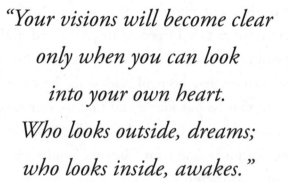

"Your visions will become clear
only when you can look
into your own heart.
Who looks outside, dreams;
who looks inside, awakes."

-CARL J. JUNG

I'VE GOT A SECRET

It aired from 1952 until 1967. It was on TV for 773 weeks with at least 672 episodes. The format changed very little. I watched from the time I played with Tinker Toys until I did junior high school homework. The show was called *I've Got a Secret*. A group of celebrity panelists tried to guess an outrageous, unpredictable, shocking, or scandalous secret that the guest lived with.

Something about the show hypnotized American folks. It was in the list of the top 30 TV shows for years. Everyone was interested in someone else's secret. The very idea that the entire nation was thinking about the same secret intrigued everybody, even me. About the only show I liked better was *Gunsmoke* because I wanted to know how Matt Dillon would find a way out of the mess he was in that week.

Maybe we liked *I've Got a Secret* because it reflected the truth about all of us. That was also the reason we played another silly game in elementary school. We would get into a circle, and I would whisper a secret to the first person, who would whisper it to the next, and so forth until it went all the way around the circle. What came back to me had nothing to do with what I whispered.

Once I whispered, "My dog has fleas." By the time it went through thirty second-graders, it came back to me as, "My mom eats peas." The secret got messed up long before it went around the circle to me. That silly game reminds me of why we often do not share our secrets. We are afraid of opening up because what we tell one person gets magnified, distorted, and misrepresented until we would not recognize it six gossipy conversations later. We all know folks who magnify anything they hear. You whisper a story into their ear, and they use a megaphone to tell the next person. Who does not know of lifelong character assassination because someone distorted a story?

Sixty percent say they have at least one secret they do not want people to know about....

Sometimes secrets do not amount to anything. Do you remember the one-time syndicated television program, *The Mystery of Al Capone's Vaults?* Geraldo Rivera had millions glued to the TV in 1986 when he promised to open the private vault of the famous gangster. What would be in it? Nothing! It looked like a mostly empty trash can. We at least expected something interesting. So, not every "secret" is a big deal.

Sixty percent say they have at least one secret they do not want people to know about, and the average person has kept it for fifteen years. Here is one poll of the top ten secrets hidden by people:

1. An affair,
2. An embarrassing incident,
3. Your web-browsing history,
4. Debt,
5. Sexual fetishes,
6. Something in your family history,
7. A phobia,
8. Something you bought,
9. That you smoke, or used to, and
10. Someone you're in love with.[1]

Most folks reading this page probably hide one or more of these very same things. Or you may have your own list.

We have secrets because we like to live behind what the psychologist Carl Jung called our *persona,* which refers to a mask, a façade, or a veneer. Folks, it means we like to look one way on the surface while what is hiding inside of us is something else. Everybody has a persona. If we did not, all of life would an endless soap opera or one episode after another of *The Jerry Springer Show.* Nobody could stand it. If people did not

---

1 http://mychannel957.com/ten-most-common-secrets-people-keep/ accessed January 19, 2016

have a *persona,* every Monday morning at the office would go something like this:

"Morning, Fred."

"Hi, Joe. How did the weekend go?"

"I got drunk and had a fight with my wife. I roared off in the car and blew last week's paycheck at a casino in Shreveport."

"Oh well, that's nothing. I embezzled five grand from my father-in-law and paid off a payday loan I took to get dope."

"How's the wife, Dan?"

"Great. She locked me out of the bedroom all weekend after a fight. How about Helen?"

"Wonderful. I surprised her while she was texting the guy she works with at the hospital, and it wasn't about work!"

No office, school, or factory would survive very long if everybody at work coughed up what is behind his or her *persona* every day. It's just too intense. That is why we need a *persona.* It lubricates life and makes things go a little smoother. We would be walking disasters without a *persona.*

All of us who pastor know something about a *persona.* As speakers and public people, we have to have one. When we stand before people who expect us to encourage them, we cannot discourage them. People give the pastor a salary or a speaker an honorarium to ring the bell, hit a home run, or at least get the bat on the ball and hit a single. We cannot strike out.

Consider what would happen if I got up and said, "Folks, I've been on the road for twenty days. I have had to deal with some crazy people who would drive most of you out of your minds. On top of that, I have had a toothache for ten days with no way to fix it until I got home. The dentist told me on the phone I needed a root canal, so I need you to buy a lot of my DVD's, CD's, and books tonight." Of course I cannot get up and say that. Instead, I must have a persona, the mask we all wear that makes life work.

You do not want the surgeon to tell you just before you go under the knife that his wife is divorcing him and making a killing. You would not want to be rolled into the operating room with him cracking up because she is buying a condo in Gulf Shores, Alabama, with your Blue Cross Blue Shield insurance. Heck, I would jump off the operating table and tell him to come back when he had it together.

The problems come, however, when we never break that *persona* with anyone, never get real with a single soul, and go to our grave with a life of unconfessed secrets. That makes folks physically, mentally, and spiritually sick. David put it this way after he committed adultery with Bathsheba and killed her husband Uriah to cover it up: "When I kept silence, my bones roared." David meant that his secret made him sick. He hid behind the *persona* of being the greatest king ever, the biggest deal in the Middle East. While he played that role, he was so sick inside that he felt as if a monster was crushing his bones with its tenacious tentacles.

The Old Testament prophet Ezekiel was one of the weird characters of the Bible. The stuff that happened to him could be on the Syfy cable channel. I call Ezekiel 8 the "Beam Me Up, Scotty" chapter. Ol' Zeke is sitting with the deacons in a prayer meeting when suddenly God beamed him up. When he landed, he was five hundred miles away in Jerusalem, at the site of what was left of Solomon's temple. God took him on a guided tour. I guess it could have been a MasterCard commercial because it was priceless.

> *The seventy men with a secret were the very leaders of the people of God. They thought they could keep their stuff a secret in the dwelling place of the living God, the holy shrine of His chosen people.*

God showed Ezekiel a hole in the wall in one of the temple rooms (Ezekiel 8:8). God told Ezekiel to dig through the hole in the wall. When he did, he found a secret door. After he went in, he found the "Hole in the Wall Gang." (Now, that was not the famous Wild West gang who stayed in the hideout in the Big Horn Mountains in northern Wyoming. That was Butch Cassidy, the Sundance Kid, Tall Texan, and "Flat Nose" Curry.) Ezekiel found seventy elders of God's covenant people hiding behind the hole in the wall of the temple within their own little cubicles. Inside the cubicle each one of them had his own secret gods and goddesses, along with incense burners to blow smoke in the dark so no one could see his secrets. And all of this was taking place in God's house. These were leaders of God's people in God's house hiding stuff they did not want anyone to see.

When you read the rest of the chapter, you'll observe that things only got worse. By the end of the chapter, they were living in open rebellion against God. What began with secrets ended with open defection (v. 16). What began in secret eventually erupted into a public repudiation of God Himself. Secrets have a way of doing that.

Please notice that this was not a group of Philistine pagans in a temple of Baal. The seventy men with a secret were the very leaders of the people of God. They thought they could keep their stuff a secret in the dwelling place of the living God, the holy shrine of His chosen people. That is why Ezekiel was beamed up and then down—to surprise them in the very act.

I wonder how many people come to God's house every Sunday hiding secrets in their hearts that no one else knows. I used to daydream about the weekly church paper years ago when I was involved in its publication. I wondered what it would be like if a church paper reported what was actually going on in the life of the church instead of all the constant happy talk. Thank God, those papers are gone now. But back in the day, the pastor had to write a column, the minister of music wrote a story, the youth minister wrote about the next crazy things the youth group would do, and the minister of education would promote the upcoming Sunday school contest. The church cook even wrote about what we would be serving for supper on Wednesday night. Yes, sometimes my mind wondered what it would be like if the church paper printed what was really going on in the life of the church:

Pastor's Column — *Sunday night was a real scene at the parsonage. My oldest daughter stomped out of the house because I missed her dance recital due to my attendance at the Brotherhood meeting. She stole the car keys and disappeared all night. I was afraid to call the sheriff since I did not want you folks to know about it. She finally came back Tuesday. Otherwise, it was a great Sunday, and the Lord blessed us with three additions to the church.*

Worship Leader's Weekly Lyrics — *Wednesday night after choir rehearsal, Suzie Kaboom helped me put away the music for the Christmas pageant. She started crying for no reason I knew. Then she spilled the beans. Her husband sneaked off to Vegas after saying he was going to a sales convention. He blew their kid's college fund at the blackjack table because he thought he could win splitting threes. He lost so much money that in desperation he doubled down on the last hand and lost it all. He had to take a bus home. The Devil made me hold Suzie ten seconds too long because she was crying so hard. Otherwise, we are having a great series of rehearsals for the pageant.*

Youth Minister's Notes – Joshua Beirbom came to the Wednesday night youth Bible study high on dope. He kept saying things off topic, and one of deacon Chad Foxworth's sons bullied him. I had to break up a fight right in the middle of our study of Revelation 19. Other than that, our youth group is growing every Wednesday, although Joshua has been asked not to come back for a while.

Minister of Education News – Last Sunday was High Attendance Day. Although our records secretary only recorded 545 people who came to Bible study, I padded the numbers to say that there were actually 605 in attendance. Anything under 600, and I know the pastor would not be happy and then breathe down my throat. I'm getting three different anxiety medications from three different doctors who all happen to be members of the church, just to handle the pressure he puts on me. I hope they don't

start talking to each other. It's all I can do to make
it from week to week.

Those are columns you will never see in the church paper. You would have to dig through holes in the walls of folks' hearts to find those secrets. Church has become a place where nearly everybody's secrets are safely hidden away. The last thing you would ever see is a report in the church paper about what is really going on.

Yet, is this really what God intended, or are we all members of the church "Hole in the Wall Gang?"

Sometimes I think the whole church got stuck in an episode of *I've Got a Secret*. Do you remember what kept everybody watching that show? At the very end the contestant had to break the *persona* and confess who he or she really was. The mask had to come off. The guard had to drop. Folks would sit around their living rooms watching the old black-and-white TV with the rabbit-ear antenna and tell one another, "Well, I'll be. I never thought about that." But today, we all play the same game.

SEARCHING THROUGH OUR SECRETS

1. Ask yourself to identify the way you maintain a *persona* and with whom you drop the mask and become a person.

2. Where are individuals most likely to keep on a mask? How do we devise the masks we wear? What is the cost of never taking them off?

3. Remember a time when you caught someone with his or her mask off. Perhaps it was a lie in the office, an adulterous affair you discovered, or an addiction you stumble upon in another person's life. How did you react, inwardly and outwardly?

4. Recall stories from the Bible and history in which persons were unmasked. Consider those narratives and meditate on the consequences.

5. How do you determine the appropriate time and person for lowering your own mask? What are the risks?

6. Do you live with a sense of superiority that you have nothing to hide, or do you become vulnerable enough to strip off the veneer and drop the façade?

NO MORE SECRETS

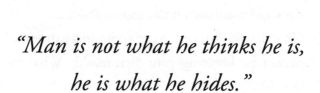

"Man is not what he thinks he is,

he is what he hides."

-Andre Malraux

Chapter Two

NECESSARY CATHARSIS

John R. Claypool (1930-2005) was a Southern Baptist preacher who later became an Episcopalian priest. Most of us thought John marched to the beat of a different drummer. He told some stories that stick to your mind like Super Glue. When John was a young preacher, he was working at a prison facility. He was something of a chaplain. There was one man whom every guard and psychiatrist thought was beyond help—incorrigible. They had all given up on him. In one more attempt, they handed him over to the young preacher.

John sat across a metal table from the prisoner. There was an ashtray, a notepad, and a pen. Not knowing anything else to do, the youthful Baptist preacher asked the hardened convict to write down what was troubling him. The prisoner filled page after page with awful, unmentionable, hateful, and dirty stuff. John was shocked. He had expected a few incoherent sentences at best, but instead, he got a notepad full of garbage.

What to do next? Since there was a lighter and ashtray on

the table, John intuitively took the pages of pain and tore them into little strips. He then took the lighter and set them on fire while repeating the words of 1 John 1:9: "If we confess our sins, He is faithful and just to forgive our sins and cleanse us from all unrighteousness." The two watched the papers burn to ashes. That was it.

But that was not it. From that day forward, the prisoner began to get better. Wholeness started to come back into his fractured life. He actually got better. There is something about getting it out, which produces catharsis.

A SPIRITUAL CATHETER

There is a group of words that belong together: catheter, catharsis, and cathartic. Two are nouns and one is an adjective. Needless to say, I have visited hundreds of hospital rooms. A significant number of folks had a catheter. We don't really talk about catheters a lot. I don't think I have ever even heard a sermon illustration about a catheter. Uncle Bud would not say at Thanksgiving dinner, "Maud, how is your catheter doing?" When you go into a hospital room, you do not remark about a catheter. You must look the other way, ask how the hospital food is, talk about the weather, pray, and then leave.

And yet catheters save lives. Many surgeries would be deadly without a catheter. Catheters carry away waste. If that physical waste was not removed, it would threaten life itself. The word comes from a Greek word that I memorized at Baylor when studying Greek with Dr. Richard Cutter. (He was a character. He would throw an eraser at you if you did not parse a verb right.) *Katharzo* is a Greek verb that means "to cleanse." From that verb we got all of the aforementioned words, and some others too. When you "cauterize" a wound, for example, you burn it to cleanse it.

Catharsis indeed saves physical lives, but it saves psychological and spiritual lives as well. What John Claypool did with the prisoner offered a moment of spiritual catharsis that touched the man's soul. We need to remember that the very word *psychology* combines the Greek words for *soul* and *knowledge*. Psychology actually began as knowledge about the soul, the very center of the center.

When I was a doctoral student at Southwestern Seminary, our cohort had a discussion about catharsis. One of the guys did a lexical study and told us that it meant "an emptying of the bowels." That was over the top for us sitting in the middle of a heavy theological discussion. We laughed our heads off. Doctoral work is tense and competitive. It seems like it will never end and wears you out. That outrageous remark became an occasion for catharsis that we needed. The very idea of saying that in the middle of a seminary theological discussion made us howl with laughter. Every time that word came up for the remainder of the term, we had another catharsis.

All of us need to be cleansed at the center. Jesus said it best, as always: "What goes into a person does not defile the person but what comes out of the person" (Matthew 15:11). When we walk around with secrets, we need a catharsis. That does not mean we have to wash our dirty linen in front of everybody. We will look at that in a later chapter. Telling the wrong people at the wrong time only complicates things. Yet, at the right time with the right person(s), you need a spiritual catharsis. The secrets have to come out, or they will poison you.

A BUMP IN THE HEAD

One of the most famous professors at Southwestern was Dr. John Drakeford. He was an Aussie psychologist who combined ministry and a counseling program he called "Integrity Therapy." He told a story called "Keeping it Under Your Hat."[2] A Jewish couple in World War II were living under the Nazi regime in Germany, expecting any day to be arrested and placed in a concentration camp. They had a paralyzed son and needed to provide care for him, so they made a deal with a one-legged man to take care of their son in exchange for the right to live in their apartment. Soon they were arrested and taken to a camp. The man who was supposed to care for their son whisked him

---

2 John W. Drakeford, *Integrity Therapy: A New Directory in Psychotherapy* (Nashville: Broadman Press, 1967), p. 34.

away to a mountain cabin, leaving him with only a little food to face certain death.

The one-legged man convinced himself that he had fulfilled his responsibility, so he subleased the apartment to add insult to injury. One day he noticed a bump the size of a pigeon's egg on his forehead. He pressed the bump and it disappeared, but then it reappeared on the back of his skull. He gave it another punch, and it came out over his ear. He pressed it there, and it showed up on top of his head. He thought that was best because he could cover it with his hat. In the same way, secrets pop up long after you think you are safe from anyone finding out.

Somewhere back there I had to read Edgar Allan Poe's story, "The Tell-Tale Heart."[3] He could scare you on a good day. Late at night, Poe can keep you awake. The narrator told the story of an old man living near him who looked at him the wrong way. He got obsessed about the old man, so he sneaked into his room, killed him, cut him into pieces, and buried him beneath the floor of his apartment. Shortly after that, the police came and told the killer that someone had heard a noise and wondered if anything was wrong. Suddenly, he heard the beating of a heart from under his floor. The police could not hear anything. The killer confessed because his conscience heard the beating of a heart even though no one else could hear it. Of course, the heart was not beating, but the sound was in his guilty head.

---

3 http://www.enotes.com/topics/tell-tale-heart

Poe was pointing out the power of secrets. The guilty man heard something that was not there. He was running away from his own shadow. The secret came out when he thought there was not even a remote chance of it being discovered.

Shakespeare put it another way:

> *Though it long sleep, the venom of great guilt*
> *When Death, or Danger, or Detection comes,*
> *Will bite the Spirits fiercely.*

What the bard meant was clear. When you think your secret was buried deep long ago, three things can unearth it quickly. When people face death, secrets tend to come to the surface. When they are in a dangerous situation, secrets rise to the top. Or when someone may have detected the secret, it brings the thing back to life. Secrets are like the one-legged man's bump on the head or Poe's heart beating under the floor: they have more lives than a cat.

KRYPTONITE FOR SECRETS

When I was a little boy in the fifties, we had a whole block filled with kids playing Superman. Mom would pin an old bath towel on my shoulders, and, like the others, I would run around jumping off of stuff. Only one thing could stop us, however.

One kid would run out with the tube from inside the paper towels and yell, "Kryptonite!" We all knew that was the end of Superman, and we would fall over, robbed of all our powers.

Secrets are the bumps on our head and the hearts under our floorboards. So what can rob secrets of their power over us?

Tell your secret to the right person. A pastor, a reliable friend, a counselor, or another professional is the kryptonite for your secret. Secrets lose their power when you get them out of your mouth and into the right person's ear. Amazing things happen when secrets come out. Your conscience is quieter. Your fellowship with God is sweeter. The monkey is off your back. Your soul has a catharsis. I can tell you about that from my own family.

MY FAMILY SECRET

"Swanberg" is a Swedish name. My grandfather, Elof Swanberg, emigrated from Sweden with his sister, Ellen, in 1912. They sailed on the Cunard ocean liner, *RMS Lusitania*. (The sinking of that ship in 1915 by a German submarine contributed to the beginning of World War I.) The two orphans had come from an affluent family, but the first father died and then the second step-father died. Their bereft mother took in sewing in order to keep body and soul together. Then, to add tragedy upon tragedy, the mother died when Elof was fourteen. Without parents, alone and desperate, the two sailed to America under the required sponsorship of a distant uncle. From the ice of Sweden they eventually found their way to the heat of central Texas in a colony called New Sweden near Manor, Texas, east of Austin. They must have been bewildered.

The uncle required my grandfather to labor for him for ten years (somewhat like an indentured servant) to compensate him for bringing the two of them from Sweden and keeping them. Grandpa Elof always had a good attitude about it and was happy to have "a roof over his head." At twenty-four years of age, he was a free man and able to start a new life in the New World. Braving the Texas storms and heat, he became a share-cropper. That meant he worked another man's land and gave the landlord one-third of the income from the crop. Then FDR, with the Farmer Fund program that changed the lives of many young farmers, offered a hundred acres on a forty-year-loan at the grand interest of .25%, one-quarter of a penny on a dollar! He got a farm, a barn, and a house. Like many a Texan who benefited from that farm bill, Elof became a Democrat for life.

All was not sunshine and roses, however. In order to pay off his loan early, he worked nearby on a cotton gin, a dangerous machine that separated cotton from the seeds buried in its white fibers. (This was before OSHA discovered that these devices were disastrous for workers.) One day, while trying to separate the seeds from the cotton, his arm got caught in the blades of the machine, which ripped it from the socket.

As the machine slowly pulled his arm deeper and deeper

into the grinding gears, he called out in pain to his friend and co-worker, Lee Anderson, to turn off the powerful belts. Miraculously, and with strength he could never find again to accomplish this feat, Anderson was able to pull the belt the opposite way, which enabled my grandpa to pull his arm loose before it pulled his entire body into the massive machinery. With a sheet blocking Grandpa's view at the Elgin hospital, my dad, Floyd Leon, got there just in time to watch the doctor cut my grandpa's arm off. At forty-nine years of age, a farmer without an arm to plow his fields had to face the reality of new life with a disability.

To add woe upon woe, when he returned home, his mentally challenged hypochondriac wife blamed him for being careless.

Grandpa Elof's generation was the very opposite of today's tell-it-all, social media, tweeting, and Facebook crowd.

It is an eternal tribute to him that he stayed with her for fifty years of such abuse.

Yet Grandpa Elof lived and died with a secret. That deeply buried secret was discovered by my sister, Darlene, while doing genealogical research by correspondence with officials in Sweden. Elof's birth certificate carried a particular symbol from the Lutheran state church of Sweden indicating that he was considered "illegitimate." That is, his putative father was not really his father. For all of his hard and challenging life, he carried that secret and thought it was buried with him in the tough Texas soil.

Grandpa Elof's generation was the very opposite of today's tell-it-all, social media, tweeting, and Facebook crowd. When I asked him about his life, he stoically responded, "Why talk about something so horrible?" All we know about him came from his sister and family. Who knows how much pain the scarlet letter cost him in his private life? Yet, just to be alive is to be legitimate. We hurt people beyond belief when we label them, brand them, or tattoo them with words that destroy and diminish and demean.

My grandpa should have known that we would have loved him even more had he told us his secret. What a catharsis it would have been and what a cleansing freedom he would have experienced if the wound had been lanced. He lived with a poison for which we could have supplied the antidote. I am certain that the Lord Jesus and a great cloud of witnesses have now told him how much we loved him and that we would have loved him even more.

SEARCHING THROUGH OUR SECRETS

1. Have you ever experienced a spiritual catharsis? What led you to that moment? How did you feel after the secret was told?

2. Have you ever helped someone else arrive at a moment of catharsis, or do you need to help someone do so?

3. Have you encountered a personal, family, or friend situation in which a secret was discovered that they did not expect to be exposed? What happened?

4. What should families do with secrets that are outed after someone dies? For example, it is not uncommon for longtime secret romantic interests to show up at funerals, to the surprise of surviving spouses. How could that be handled? Should family members be protected?

5. Can you imagine a different outcome for Elof's situation? Could you narrate to yourself a creative ending of that story that involves a cathartic moment of disclosure?

6. Do you firmly believe you can even tell God your secrets and receive His grace?

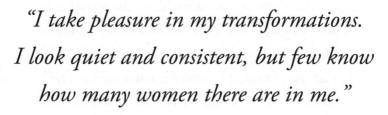

"I take pleasure in my transformations.
I look quiet and consistent, but few know
how many women there are in me."

-ANAIS NIN

CHAPTER 3

ME AND MY SHADOW

Frank Sinatra sang it. So did Sammy Davis Jr. You can also add Judy Garland and Perry Como. Now, unless you are just a little younger than I am, you may not even remember some of those folks. For you "millennials," you can listen to Frank and Sammy sing it on YouTube.[4] Fifty years ago, most Americans who watched one of the three TV networks (that was all the choice we had) could sing along with it:

> Like the wallpaper sticks to the wall
> Like the seashore clings to the sea
> Like you'll never get rid of your shadow
> Frank, you'll never get rid of me
>
> Let all the others fight and fuss
> Whatever happens, we've got us.

---

4 https://www.youtube.com/watch?v=e5hXtGkzZ9k accessed February 4, 2016

Me and my shadow
We're closer than pages that stick in a book
We're closer than ripples that play in a brook
Strolling down the avenue
Wherever you find him, you'll find me, just look
Closer than a miser or the bloodhounds to Liza

Me and my shadow
We're closer than smog when it clings to L.A.
We're closer than Bobby is to J.F.K.
Not a soul can bust this team in two
We stick together like glue

And when it's sleeping time
That's when we rise
We start to swing
Swing to the skies
Our clocks don't chime
What a surprise
They ring-a-ding-ding!
Happy New Year!

Me and my shadow
And now to repeat what I said at the start
They'll need a large crowbar to break us apart
We're alone but far from blue.[5]

---

5 www.azlyarics.com/lyrics/franksinatra/meandmyshadow.html accessed February 4, 2016.

The lyrics referred to two friends who were always together. In this case it was two members of the famous Rat Pack— Sammy Davis Jr. and Frank Sinatra. Choir boys they were not. Together, they were infamous.

Yet, in another sense it could be a song about any of us or all of us. In the words of psychiatrist Carl Jung, all of us have a "shadow." *That* shadow is not a friend who sticks as close to us as a shadow. It is certainly not the shadow we cast on the sidewalk or wall. For Jung, that shadow is a metaphor for everything about us that we hide in the dark, repress, deny, or don't want other people to see. In fact, we even project it onto other people as if the shadow belonged to them rather than to us.

Believe me, I am not a psychiatrist, although some folks who listen to me think I need one. Did you hear the joke about the man who came into the shrink's office wearing only Saran Wrap? The doctor said, "I can clearly see you are crazy." Another one says, "Do you know how many psychiatrists it takes to change a light bulb? Only one, but the bulb has really got to want to change." Then there's the one which says, "My psychiatrist sent me for an MRI because she thinks I have a magnetic personality." One more: A while back I told the shrink that every time I drink a cup of coffee, I get a stabbing pain in my right eye. He asked, "Did you try taking the spoon out?" (That cost me $200.)

But I do have some sense of folks in the Bible who had a shadow self. Jesus met a man with a whole lot of shadows, as recorded in Mark 5. We call him the Gerasene demoniac. He lived in a cemetery not far from the shore of the Sea of Galilee. For Jews, that was horrible because a cemetery was an unclean place. But that was just the beginning of his problems. He was isolated because no one wanted to get close to him. He was self-destructive in that he cut himself with jagged stones. He was uncontrollable, so no chains forged in the nearby town could control him.

> *If we cannot get rid of our secret, we try to get rid of ourselves by doing something that numbs us, amuses us, or makes us forget who we are.*

I can imagine a Galilean family trying to take a picnic, and suddenly this ghoulish guy ran out of the cemetery and terrorized everyone. Maybe a young couple was walking along the shore, and the dude was about to pop the question when suddenly there was a screaming naked man running out of the graveyard crying, "Whaaaaaaaaaaaaagagagaga." That would surely break up a proposal.

Then the demoniac met Jesus. Jesus asked him the well-known question, "What is your name?" He gave just as well-known an answer: "Legion." The poor dude had watched the Roman legions march on the nearby great road. There were about five thousand men in a Roman legion. As he cut himself with rocks and ran around like the original streaker in the tombs, an idea took hold of him. He felt like there were five thousand different people, or shadows, lurking inside of him. He was full of shadow selves. He was the original "knock, knock joke." Someone could have said, "Knock, knock. Who's there?" He would have responded, "Five thousand of us."

Now, make no mistake about it. This man was demon possessed. That is a reality, and something you do not want to mess with. Yet living with secrets inside of us can make us feel similar to this man. Just as he was isolated, our secrets also isolate us. To live with a secret inside of us is to be like Dr. Jekyll and Mr. Hyde. We act one way at one time and another way some other time. We are always having to hide the secret, and in some mysterious way, that cuts us off from other people.

Bernie Madoff is considered by many to be the criminal of our times. He was ripping off his own friends for millions, and not one of his closest associates or family members understood the gigantic fraud he was committing. I bet you Bernie did not have any close friends because carrying a secret always keeps you on guard.

Secrets also make us self-destructive. We may not cut ourselves with rocks, but we may pierce ourselves in other ways. Secrets have a sneaky tendency to make us drink stuff, take stuff, or do stuff that violates us. We can't get the secret out of us, so we literally do something to take ourselves "out of it." If we cannot get rid of our secret, we try to get rid of ourselves by doing something that numbs us, amuses us, or makes us forget who we are. The man whose marriage is falling apart often acts out in secret ways that would really make it fall apart. The alcoholic woman spends an enormous amount of time trying to conceal her bottles and habit or undo the damage she has done to her closest relationships. All of this is the equivalent of cutting herself with chains and stones.

Sometimes the best way to get rid of our shadows is to help others with theirs.

"Who knows what evil lurks in the hearts of man? The Shadow knows." This famous phrase came from Pulp Fiction in the thirties and forties. The latest appearance of The Shadow was in a 1994 movie featuring the fictional character, Lamont Cranston, played by Alec Baldwin. Under the tutelage of a saintly man, Cranston is freed from the dark forces that overtook him in World War I. He returns to New York City under the guise of a playboy but uses his power to undermine the underworld. When he does what he does, all that can be seen is his shadow. In a sense, his dangerous and malevolent shadow becomes a force for good.

The same can be true for any of us. Once freed from the tyranny of our shadow selves, we are at peace with ourselves. Our shadows are tamed, our secrets are told, and the very thing that ruined us can become the thing that saves others. No one, for instance, can help another porn addict like someone who has overcome porn and now lives a pure life. Who can help a drug addict like someone who has conquered dope? Who can strengthen a friend's failing marriage like a couple who has been on the brink of divorce but then returned to a healthy marriage? In each of these instances, a secret shadow can be turned into light.

By saving others, you may also save yourself. Someone told of a man who intended to commit suicide by jumping off the long pier in Gulfport, Mississippi. He was practicing his jump just to get up the nerve to kill himself. Just before he jumped, however, he heard someone in the breakers below screaming, "Help, help! I'm drowning!" He reasoned that if he was going to commit suicide, he should just as well jump in and try to save the drowning man. He would be no worse off and might save somebody before he drowned. So he jumped. With a few sure, swift swimmer's strokes, he saved the drowning man. By the time he got the man back to the beach, he had forgotten all about his own troubles and felt a new purpose for living.

> *We all are recovering from something.*

Sometimes the best way to get rid of our shadows is to help others with theirs. Getting out of your own secrets and helping others who are hurting in different ways can release you from your shadows.

It's just like the story of my sons, Dustin and Chad. They have learned the secret of helping themselves by helping others. When they go to AA and Celebrate Recovery meetings, and even participate in interventions, what they do to help *others* stay sober helps *them* stay sober.

Even their dad has been helped by overhearing what they are doing for others. And now you are being encouraged because they encouraged me while encouraging someone else. This circle is enlarging all of the time! Remember this, WE ARE ALL RECOVERING FROM SOMETHING. It may be childhood abuse, bullying, betrayal, failure in a way we thought we would never fail, or a thousand other things. By helping others with the same thing, we learn to stay clear of it ourselves. When we are surrounded by light on every side, it does not cast a shadow.

SEARCHING THROUGH OUR SECRETS

1. Jung's concept of the "shadow self" speaks to something in most of us.. What are the shadows that live in your own life?

2. For many of us, our strengths are also our weaknesses. For example, an assertive person in business may also be a bully at home. What strengths in your life project a shadow of the opposite weakness?

3. What have you overcome in your own life that enables you to encourage someone struggling with the same thing?

4. Similar to Legion, how many different beings live inside you?

5. Have you ever overcome your own problems by helping someone else live redemptively with their problems?

6. What have you bragged you would never, ever do? Why did you say that?

NO MORE SECRETS

"*Secrets, silent, stony, sit in the dark palaces of both our hearts: secrets weary of their tyranny; tyrants willing to be dethroned.*"

-James Joyce

Chapter 4

Bugs, Rocks,
and the Power of Light

CONSIDERATION: HOW WILL
MY SECRET AFFECT OTHERS?

Do you remember your first cell phone? Actually, they were first called "car phones" because that is where most people used them. They were huge! You had to lift weights to be able to hold one up to your ear. When they first became popular about 1985, people who could not afford a cell phone would buy a fake one to impress others.

You may also remember something else. I sure do. The early technology was poor, so the bandwidth was not sufficient and one call would bleed into another. All of a sudden, while driving down the road, you would hear someone else's conversation. I remember a real doozy:

"Well, if that's what you're going to do, I'm going to tell everybody at the office."

"Ha, if you do that, I'll call your wife and tell her about the trip to Kansas City."

"If you say a word about that, I'll show the boss your fake expense report."

And so forth. You get the idea. I was talking to my sweetheart, and suddenly I was overhearing an entirely different conversation.

It's funny to say that this phenomenon is a lot older than cell phones. In the Old West, they first strung a transcontinental telegraph line in 1861. President Lincoln received the first message. Yet shortly after that, there was confusion because one wire would cause a nearby one to vibrate. They had not counted on that kind of mix-up. The message on one wire would mess up the message on another.

Not only are cell phones and telegraph wires like that, but also human beings. What we think is hidden causes mixed spiritual signals in other people—and they may not even know what is going on. That is the lesson in the biblical story of Achan. His name always reminded me of "Ashcan." He certainly trashed the victory of God's people in the battle for Ai.

It happened like this: At the critical battle of Jericho, Joshua told God's people that everything they took at Jericho—all of the booty and spoils of war—belonged to God. The next battle on God's agenda was at the Canaanite city of Ai. But the leaders of God's army were cocky and self-sufficient. They told

Joshua to send a fraction of the army (Joshua 7:3) because they thought this would be a simple clean-up operation compared to Jericho. What a surprise! The Ai army turned into a battalion of Rambos. They chased the superior Hebrew army across the desert and humiliated them. Joshua was crushed.

Then God told Joshua what had happened. One Hebrew man had taken some of the Jericho loot and hid it in his tent even though it was supposed to be devoted to God. It belonged to the LORD, and He is serious about His stuff.

Joshua 7 is a dramatic detective story. It reminds me of one of the forensic shows on TV now. God narrows the field to find who did it.

Achan's secret buried underneath his tent caused the defeat of the entire Hebrew army.

God exposes one tribe (Judah) and then one family in that tribe (the Zarhites). He narrows it down even further to one member of that family—Zabdi. Finally, they fingered his grandson, Achan. He had hidden a Jericho Versace suit, a pile of Jericho Tiffany silver, and a chunk of Jericho gold under his tent (v. 21). Joshua acted swiftly. Achan and all he had, even his donkeys, were stoned in the desert and then burned. Tough stuff. It's tight, but it's right. You can read it and weep. Nevertheless, God is serious when your secret messes up the victory of His people.

We do not know how or why, but Achan's secret buried underneath his tent caused the defeat of the entire Hebrew army.

God had pulled off an exodus, given them His commandments, rained manna on the people, and given them clothes and shoes that would not wear out for forty years. Yet this one doofwad, Achan, almost derailed the whole thing.

Secrets hurt. Secrets derail things. Secrets defeat the larger purposes of God. Achan's hidden sinful conversation confused Joshua's godly leadership. The stuff buried under one tent defeated an entire army.

> *What if any of us had the worst three minutes of our thought life projected on one of the large high-definition screens of the church sanctuary?*

There is a great spiritual principle here: "A little leaven leavens the whole lump" (1 Corinthians 5:6; Galatians 5:9). A chemist once described the process of leavening. A piece of leaven no bigger than one three-thousandth of an inch begins to move about in all directions. It develops tiny projectiles, which break off and become new independent pieces of leaven. It is like a sci-fi thriller. Soon they are everywhere, leavening the dough.

Secrets are just like that. A tiny spiritual secret can spawn more spiritual secrets, and soon secrets are everywhere. Secrets take on a life of their own and breed more secrets. We sweep a little stuff under the floor mat while we keep everything else spotless.

A husband opens a secret bank account that his wife does not know about, but he forgets that a bank statement comes in the mail to the house. His wife then wonders what else he is hiding. A junior executive cuts a corner that saves his company a million bucks, but it lands the company in a nasty lawsuit. His co-workers wonder what else he has swept under the mat. So, even little things can undo you if they are hidden. My dad, Floyd Leon, put it this way: "You can change your character overnight, but not your reputation."

MY OWN BATTLES

As a traveling Christian speaker, I have secrets. Even at my age, I fight the battles of a teenager. Things I saw years ago pop back into my head. I deal with lust, just like every man. I have memories of past images while walking through airports, standing on stages, and spending nights in lonely hotels that all look boringly the same. How many times flipping through the television channels have I inadvertently discovered something that would make Hugh Hefner blush? By God's grace, I have never sinned in a scandalous publicized way, nevertheless, I still sin in the flesh and in thought.

At my ManCode conferences, I put it this way: What if any of us had the worst three minutes of our thought life projected on one of the large high-definition screens of the church sanctuary? Most of us would have to move to Australia at the far end of the outback—and that does not mean a steak house.

That is not to mention the thoughts that come into our heads while watching an R-rated movie or taking a lingering look at an attractive woman in an airport, church service, or mall. Such temptations are cancerous to the spirit, toxic to the life of an authentic man, and poisonous to the prayer life. Even seemingly innocent activities with persons of the opposite sex can lead to an attack of unsolicited thoughts of lust.

> *We must have men with whom we share these common temptations who can both understand and challenge us.*

Such things harm the spirit, infect the soul, and limit the life of prayer. James, the younger half-brother of the Lord, wrote, "The effective fervent prayer of a righteous man availeth much" (James 5:16). Even entertaining evil thoughts makes our prayers bounce off the ceiling like BB's and deafens us to the voice of God speaking to us. Because of that, we need to have some buddies who will hold us accountable. We must have men with whom we share these common temptations who can both understand and challenge us. Our wives, girlfriends, and sisters may have no idea of the lustful possibilities that can haunt even the best of us men, and we cannot tell them without possible hurt and misunderstanding.

Paul wrote Timothy, "Flee youthful lusts" (2 Timothy 2:22). He did not write Timothy to pray about them, ponder them, analyze them, or dwell on them. Instead, he said, "FLEE." There are times when the only solution is a good pair of Nikes. When Potiphar's wife tried to seduce Joseph, he ran rather than ponder the situation.

If you wanted to hire a driver to drive you up a narrow one-lane road high in the Andes Mountains with a sheer drop-off of two thousand feet, would you ask for a driver who could drive as close to the edge as possible? Would you ask him to keep half of the wheel over the edge in thin air? Probably not. You would want a driver who hugged the side of the mountain and stayed as far from the edge as possible. Go then and do likewise.

STRANGE THINGS IN THE CHURCH

A friend of mine was called to his seminary pastorate, a small church in a one-horse town. The second Sunday morning, while standing at the church door, he was receiving the usual platitudes about his sermon: "You sure stepped on our toes . . . . You are the next Billy Graham . . . . That was a great word. . . ." Then a young deacon who had served on the pulpit committee blurted out at the door, "What are you going to do about our mess?" The young student pastor had never heard of "the mess."

"The whole county is talking about it," retorted the deacon. "Our church is a laughing stock all over the county." Even though that same young deacon had been on the pastor search committee, he had failed to tell the young pastor about the "problem."

The new pastor made an appointment with the young deacon. As they sat in the small living room of the rural house, the young deacon revealed, "It's about wife-swapping. We've got two couples in the church who are swingers. One of them sits in the choir and winks at the other one in the pew." The neophyte pastor thought to himself that he wished the deacon would have told him that before he came to the church.

After weeks of negotiations, private conversations, small-group discussions, and whispering sessions in the hallways of the church, the young pastor called a deacon's meeting at 3 p.m. on Sunday afternoon. (That's always a bad idea because it's during a football game, but that's another matter altogether.) He mildly asked the deacons if they would send a letter to the two couples asking them to consider their ways. One of the older deacons stood up and said, "Well, are you going to write me a letter every time I sin?" The young pastor was dumbfounded. That kind of small-town, home-grown, corn-pone wisdom flummoxed him. He did not know what to say. The meeting was dismissed, nothing was done, and the "secret" continued.

The power of secrets is just like that: as long as they are secrets, they have their power.

The young pastor saw what a secret can do—mysteriously. Little by little, similar sins having to do with love triangles began to infiltrate the entire church. The Spirit vanished from the church, and the power left the fellowship. Everyone knew things were wrong. All that happened could not even be told here, decades later. This was all because a group of men decided to cover up a secret.

Secrets are like the Bermuda Triangle in that they suck everything into themselves. Secrets make a family, a church, or a community become a regular *Peyton Place*. Well, if you don't remember that messy soap opera, what about *Desperate Housewives*? Life indeed becomes a reality show that reveals everything all the time. (Why do folks like those crazy shows? Maybe because it makes them feel better about their own mess.)

Dr. Charles Stanley coins some great proverbs, or "Life Principles," as they are known. One of my favorites (and the very first principle) is, "Our intimacy determines our impact." Hidden things diminish our impact. Folks looking at us do not know why, but we do. Our "power bar" in the video game of life tanks because of our secrets. Yet, our God is an expert at comebacks. Jesus was as dead as dead could be but look at what God did with Him.

BUGS UNDER THE ROCK

When I was a little boy, I liked to turn over big rocks. There were hundreds of bugs under the rocks when it was wet. When I turned a rock over, all of the bugs under the rock ran away. The light, the heat, and the sudden exposure made the bugs head for the hills. The power of secrets is just like that: as long as they are secrets, they have their power. When they are appropriately brought into the light, secrets run. You can make secrets run by getting them into the light in the right way.

The power of secrets is in their hiddenness. They are the monkey on your back. They are the pebble in your shoe. Do you remember Hans Christian Anderson's little story, "The Princess and the Pea"? A certain man wanted to marry a real princess. A visitor told him how to tell if a woman was a real princess. If he would put a pea under twenty mattresses and eiderdown covers, he would find out who the princess was. Then one night a young lady slept on the mattresses and complained that she could hardly sleep at all because of something hard under them. That was proof she was a real princess.

> *Even under all kinds of protection, we can still feel them, and they keep us awake at night. We cannot put enough on top of them to keep us from being tormented by them.*

Not to overstate the point, but that is what secrets do to those who keep them. Even under all kinds of protection, we can still feel them, and they keep us awake at night. We cannot put enough on top of them to keep us from being tormented by them. So, get rid of the pea!

My high-school English teacher put it this way: "It's not the rock in your path; it's the grain of sand in your shoe." That grain of sand can make a blister. A *Friday Night Lights* kind of running back can fail because of that grain of sand. A contestant on *Dancing with the Stars* can trip because of that little grain of sand. It's the little things that can trip us up. As Benjamin Franklin once said,

> For want of a nail, the shoe was lost. For want of the shoe, the horse was lost. For want of a horse, the rider was lost. For the want of the rider, the battle was lost. For the want of a battle, the kingdom was lost.

There was a group of monks who were known for their strict devotion and mortification of the flesh. They put peas in their shoes when they went to the fields to work all day. These peas made them terribly uncomfortable, and they grimaced and frowned all day, every day. But they knew they were mortifying their flesh. One day a smiling novice monk joined them to work in the fields. Unlike them, he was happy, smiling, singing, and joyous. A rumor started that the new monk was not following the orders to put peas in his shoes. They were whispering that this new monk was not following the strict rule of the order.

Finally, the abbot confronted him in front of all of the other monks. The abbot demanded to know if he had put the peas in his shoes. He assured the abbot that he most certainly did. The abbot and all the monks demanded to know how he could possibly look happy with peas in his shoes while working in the hot sun.

He replied, "It is simple; I boil the peas."

When you tell the secret in the right way to the appropriate people, you boil the peas!

SEARCHING THROUGH OUR SECRETS

1. When have you seen a secret derail the plans or ruin the spirit of an entire group?

2. Have you ever been in a situation with the uneasy sense that something was wrong, but you could not put your finger on what it was? Did it turn out to be someone's secret that infected the situation?

3. Do you have an accountability person/group of any kind? Is there someone to whom you can tell anything and feel secure about it?

4. Identify the places and times you are most vulnerable to temptation and hidden behavior. Do you have a strategy in advance for such situations?

5. Take a clothes hanger apart until it is a straight piece of wire. Bend it up and down to demonstrate

your thought life over a month. What does that look like?

6. Do you remember your victories over temptation? What enabled any of those victories?

NO MORE SECRETS

"*Speak the truth
even if your voice shakes.*"

SPRAY PAINTED ON THE SIDE
OF AN ABANDONED HOUSE

CHAPTER 5

ALL IN THE FAMILY

Secrets give you vertigo. Trying to make sense out of something that makes no sense makes you spiritually dizzy. Did you ever spin yourself around when you were a kid in order to make yourself dizzy? Do you remember the feeling? You spun around and your whole world would spin, too. Secrets are like that. Secrets cause you to lose balance—and everything around you as well.

Perhaps you never spun around like that as a child. But have you ever gotten one of those enormous jigsaw puzzles like "Yosemite Park in 5000 Pieces"? Maybe you got it for Christmas and started it on the dining room table. (That was your first mistake because you had to move the thing before New Year's Day.) You know what happened. You got stuck because there was one piece you had to have to finish an entire part of the puzzle. The tree needed one piece of bark, the mountain peak needed a piece of snow, or the bear needed a piece of brown fur. You knew you could not go on without that piece. You just hoped somebody on the other side of the world who packed the thing did not forget that piece. Secrets can make you feel that way. Life seems to be missing a piece, and you do not know what or where it is.

For fifteen years, every time my mother-in-law would go to Mississippi for a cherished family reunion, she would have a severe mysterious emotional reaction after the trip. What should have been a favorite memory became a nightmare. The very thing she wanted to do became the very thing that tormented her. It made her family feel like I did when I spun around as a child and everything else spun around, too.

> *You can only hold an inflated beach ball down for a second. Just when you think you have got the ball underwater, it pops up on your other side.*

My father-in-law would only tell us that his wife could not handle going back to Mississippi. That left us with a missing piece of a big puzzle. She loved her family, longed to plan trips back to Mississippi, and enjoyed the anticipation of the expected trip. She would help everyone pack, buy snacks for the road, plan where to stop on the way, and be sure the house was prepared for the family to be gone. Yet, as the piney woods of East Texas gave way to the landscape of Louisiana, a shadow started to fall.

Kids have an innate radar that senses when there is a missing piece of the puzzle. They are intuitive. They cannot name what is wrong, cannot guess what piece of the puzzle is missing, and do not even know how to express what they are feeling. But kids somehow *know*. There is the hint of a noxious odor in the air that they detect, and it makes them uneasy, anxious, and spiritually dizzy (as if they are spinning around).

Our sense of smell is the most sensitive of the five senses. We can smell many more things than we can see, taste, touch, or hear. The nose knows. It can whiff the faintest difference in the air. So is our spiritual perception of the atmosphere around us. We can tell the slightest changes, even when we cannot name them.

You can only hold an inflated beach ball down for a second. Just when you think you have got the ball underwater, it pops up on your other side. You can use both hands, sit on it, lie down on it, or ask someone to help you hold it under. But the result is always the same—it just pops back up.

The only way you can keep the beach ball underwater is by letting the air out. In the same way, when you tell the secret about something, it lets the air out.

Do you remember Bozo? He is 4'6" tall. You can still buy him at Toys-R-Us. When we were kids, we used to try to knock him over. He always came back up smiling at us. We even took a baseball bat and hit him. He just reappeared with that same silly grin. One time we decided to do surgery on Bozo just to see what was inside of him. It was a deflating experience for Bozo. We found out he had something in him we did not know about. He was weighted with stuff at the bottom that made him come back. His secret was something in him that we did not know about. That is how secrets are. They keep coming back up at you until you do the delicate surgery that lets them out.

On Christmas of 2010, my mother-in-law said she needed to speak to me. You can tell the difference when a loved one just wants to chat and when she really wants to have a heart-to-heart talk. It's in the tone of her voice and the look in her eye. We were spending Christmas at a lake resort, and one morning as I came outside, she was walking down the road to my cabin. We met in the middle of the road, and it was there that she handed me the missing piece of the puzzle. With that piece the whole picture came together.

Her mother had died of cancer when she was only five years old. She was the youngest of thirteen children. The oldest daughter was thirty years old when she was born. Her dad was way too old to care for her by himself, so she was handed off to various relatives, mainly the older siblings who were already married by this time. Her sense of worth diminished while she was passed along like a child's doll from one place to another. The ultimate security for a child, a stable and lasting home, was denied her.

Famed British poet G. K. Chesterton once compared the offspring of herrings to human children. Herrings have thousands of babies at a time, but they do not have to raise them. The herring world is very simple: eat or be eaten. But human children are not really like that at all. Because of the complexities of human life created in the image of God, it takes time to rear a child. To be passed from home to home has devastating consequences.

I listened with my heart in my throat as she began to unpack her secrets. My heart was thumping in my chest, my breath bated, and my eyes wide open. The atmosphere on that resort road was thick with significance and anticipation.

She had just started adolescence. Both a family member and a close friend of the family had sexually abused her. Trust shattered, hope fled, and dreams vanished. So, at seventeen years of age, living in a small rural Mississippi town, she saw no future. She married a vicious man who thought he could use her for his own warped ambition and manipulative advantage. Then she got pregnant. That did not fit into his perverse plans, so he insisted she have an abortion. But his family would not even pay for it.

I stood there with a lump in my throat. She had lived with all of this pain, each of these separate secrets, all a piece of a larger puzzle, for all of these years. Yet the last of the secrets was still not out. Broke, hurting, confused and terrified, she knew she must get help. An older brother thrust a fifty-dollar bill at her with disgust and blurted out, "Sister, it's your problem. Go fix it." Slinking up and down back alleys in Jackson, Mississippi, she whispered her shame to shady people, who furtively pointed her to a hack who performed the procedure. It was a debacle that might have left her without the ability to bear children.

Divorce followed and then a move to Texas. There, she met my fabulous father-in-law. Due to the clumsy abortion, she had to tell him that she might never be able to have a baby again.

He gave her great grace, along with his redemptive promise that he did not care. He just knew that he loved her and wanted to marry her, which may have been the brightest moment in her life. A minor key *life* turned into a major key *moment*. It was like the sun shining through a dark and cloudy sky.

As a mature woman, my wife Lauree recognizes that her own life was in that *moment*. Had her dad said no, closed his heart to grace, and refused to marry her mother, I would not have my wife and two wonderful sons. All of that happened in that *moment*. Sometimes God hangs the heaviest weights on the thinnest wires. When you hear someone's secret and give them grace, the whole future is in that moment. My next words to my mother-in-law were, "Kathy, I love you more now than ever before, and your family will also do the same. And Kathy, GOD LOVES YOU and your child in heaven loves YOU too."

But a secret partially told is a secret nonetheless. I told her that she needed to reveal this story to her family. The secret had been like leaven in the dough. It had sent out tentacles that affected everyone. For a reason known only to her and God, however, she could not do that.

Six days after our conversation, she had a psychiatric event that sent her to a hospital for six weeks. She never recovered to the point of the clarity she had in our previous conversation. Lauree went with her mother and dad to the psychiatrist several times. Her mother's medication and frame of mind never permitted her to tell the story in a coherent way. A moment was lost forever.

I use this phrase often when sharing her story, especially for pregnancy centers and those who counsel women about abortion: "The further down you hold a beach ball, the bigger the splash it makes when it comes to the surface." We will never know what might have happened if she had told her secret to the family openly after she whispered it to me on that eventful day.

To fast forward, she must have known when she told me her secret that she was sick and probably wouldn't live much longer. After thirty-three days in hospice care, she would not let go of life. She murmured incoherently, yet the family listened to every syllable. Even the doctor asked us if there was some reason she would not let go, some unfinished business. Finally, I had a moment with her. That moment is forever shrouded in sacred silence. In the secrecy of the confessional, that scene is locked and I have thrown away the key. A moment so sacred and a conversation so sensitive cannot be shared.

> *Your willingness to tell your secret to someone may be redemptive for some or many more.*

Suffice it so say that shortly after that, she went into the life beyond. Lauree told her what a wonderful mother she was. We gathered around her bedside and sang "Amazing Grace." She went into the life beyond, where there are no more nights and no more tears and no more pain. She lives in the light of the risen Lamb. And there she met her baby—bright, beautiful, and beaming—awaiting her for all those years.

This sacred family story is told only in outline. There are things you do not need to know. What is important is the lesson learned, the truth lived. Repressed or suppressed secrets take their toll and dizziness ensues. A piece of the puzzle is strangely missing. There are some significant lessons for all of us in this story.

Your secrets do not belong to everybody. My mother-in-law trusted me. She knew me as a person of mercy, so she felt safe in sharing with me. Everyone needs someone like that. I was close enough to have the awesome power of a listening ear, yet far enough away to be more detached than family members. I was the right person to tell.

Nevertheless, sometimes you have to move beyond telling the story to one person. We will not know until eternity what might have happened if she had been able to tell the story to everyone who needed to hear it. I suggested that she do so, but I also respected her personal choice. You cannot tell other people's secrets for them. You cannot draft, coerce, or manipulate people into telling their secrets. You can suggest and even plead, but there is a line that you cannot cross.

Your willingness to tell your secret to someone may be redemptive for some or many more. Some of you scanning this page can be liberated by reading the story. Her willingness to tell me may open up your own willingness to tell someone. Persons she never knew may be helped because she entered that sacred moment of trust.

Many cannot tell their secrets because they feel they have

committed the original sin—that no one ever did anything like them. But that is the Devil's lie. Sin is awfully repetitive and boring. If you read the Ten Commandments and the Sermon on the Mount, you will find about every variety of sin that people commit. There is very little originality in sin. One priest said that God gave the seventh commandment (against adultery) to make Catholics come to the confessional. He heard the same sad story over and over. You have not done anything or hidden anything that has not been done and hidden before.

You may object that you sinned against the great light and privilege you received. You were reared in a Christian home, your mother's milk was the Bible, and God protected you from many dangers. Yet you have secrets anyway. You are not alone. I know some of the premier Christian families in the nation, and they all have secrets. Do not make an idol out of your secret. Do not make it bigger than the grace of God. He will not get dizzy and fall off His throne when you tell your secret. God will not resign. He will not say, "I just can't take it anymore. I resign from being God." God can take it, so give it to Him.

IN THE REARVIEW MIRROR

I so wish Lauree's mom would have told us about her early life in Mississippi with its undiluted pain and perpetual remorse. But instead, she kept these secrets inside her. For my part, I would have been more gracious to her in the midst of the vertigo we all suffered because of her repressed secrets. She would have given me opportunity to express grace, and she would also have experienced grace as a result. In a sense, it was a double robbery. She robbed herself of grace much needed and then robbed us of the grace that needed to be given. I do not write that with any sense of superiority. In so many ways she was a better woman than I am a man. Yet everyone lost because of the hiddenness of her life.

Looking back, I think of the torture she must have endured listening to "right to life" sermons. She must have felt as if she were the target. I do believe in the sanctity of life, but I also believe abortion is a sin among sins and can be covered with the blood of Jesus. I think of Vestal Goodman singing, "Rock of Ages, cleft for me/Let me hide myself in Thee." Kathy needed somewhere to hide safely when she sat through such necessary but uncomfortable sermons. Then there must have been the talk in the beauty shop. Men talk about sports and politics in barber shops, but women talk about their own lives. How many times did she hear someone explode, "How could anyone abort her baby? That is murder!" She had to sit through that as those words seared her ears. If she had shared her secret with us, it would have given her a hiding place for that pain.

She might even have worked in a pregnancy center telling other troubled seventeen-year-olds about her journey from pain to recovery. By helping others, her own story might have been redemptive. Yet all of that was lost because of her silence.

What can I say about her husband and my father-in-law, George? He was a World War II veteran who kept that horror and loss bottled up inside of him. Men in his generation did that. Psychiatrists have noted that the "Ad Man" generation of gruff and blustering execs who never opened up, liked to smoke and drink, and bottled everything up inside died from unusual rates of heart attacks and stomach cancer. George did not at all do any of those things. He is a gentle, gracious, godly man. Yet he did belong to a generation of men who kept stories bottled up inside. It is a striking thing that only movies like *Saving Private Ryan* have recently enabled some of the Greatest Generation to tell stories long buried in untouched rooms of their lives. That is a reason I am honored to serve many of our military and wounded warriors in the twilight of their lives.

Yet God can bring redemption out of anything. When Nehemiah had rebuilt the walls of Jerusalem, he divided the choir into two groups, and they sang while marching around the walls. Most strikingly, they sang at the Dung Gate (Nehemiah 12:31). At the very place where the excrement was dumped from a city full of ruminating, cud-chewing animals, they stopped and sang the praises of God. If you will excuse the language, on a pile of crap that stunk to high heavens they found a place to praise God.

Life hands us a lot of dung, yet God can redeem even the Dung Gate. It was out of all of these experiences and those with our own sons that my sweet wife Lauree exclaimed, "No more secrets." That phrase led to this book and the very words you are reading. Yes, you can praise God at the dung gates of life.

The most expensive coffee in the world is Kopi Luwak. It costs from a hundred to six hundred dollars per pound, depending on the source and authenticity. Why? Civet cats eat the coffee berries. As the berries pass through the alimentary canal of the civet cat, the enzymes transform the beans into the best coffee in the world. One cup of the coffee costs from thirty-five to a hundred dollars. When the civet cat defecates, the feces contain the beans. They are extracted, washed, processed, and sold as the best coffee in the world. It is the process of going through the digestion of the civet cat that turns the dung of the cat into the very thing that carries the best coffee in the world—buried in cat crap! (Please excuse the expression, but we are all adults here.) Life hands us all degrading dung and catastrophic crap. It is God's redemptive grace that helps us digest what life feeds us, and, at the other end, uses it for redemptive purposes. That is why you have this book.

SEARCHING THROUGH OUR SECRETS

1. Do you encounter family situations that leave you wondering where the missing piece of the puzzle is? One counselor told a surprised husband, "Pray for your wife. She has great hurt to overcome." Yet neither the wife nor the counselor

said what that hurt was. How do you deal with undefined hurt?

2. What kinds of hurts do you keep hidden inside? Most hurts involve some combination of money, sex, and power. The power may have been experienced as abuse. Would you dare name those things?

3. How important is it to tell secrets before it is too late?

4. Can you let someone you know who is carrying a secret grasp the grace you would give them if they would only open up?

5. What are the effects on others, like the older generation, who live with the buried secret of another within the bounds of confidentiality?

6. What ways could God use your own pain if you opened up and shared it with others who have the same pain?

NO MORE SECRETS

"To confess your sins to God is not to tell God anything God doesn't already know. Until you confess them, however, they are the abyss between you. When you confess them, they become the bridge."

-FREDERICK BUECHNER

CHAPTER 6

CONFESSION

The practice of confession has a venerable history in the Christian church. Scholars have studied it in detail. There is some evidence in the first four centuries of the church that confession was public—to the entire assembly. Gradually the practice became private. The confessor was a priest who sat on one side of a box-like enclosure with a screen between him and the confessing Christian.

In Catholic thought, the priest "held the keys" of the church. Yet Jesus gave the keys to Peter and the apostles. He told them that whatever they bound on earth would be bound in heaven and whatever they loosed on earth would be loosed in heaven. "Binding" and "loosing" were rabbinic terms for refusing to forgive and forgiving, respectively. The Catholic Church always claimed it has the power of those keys. When you see the emblem of the pope, you'll notice it has a large set of crossed keys. The pope hands these keys down—from the cardinals to the bishops and the bishops to the individual priest. That priest has the right to declare the confessing Christian forgiven and absolved if the Christian shows true penitence.

Now, yours truly is a Baptist, but our Catholic friends have one up on us about this practice of declaring someone who tells his or her secrets to be free of them. The priest in the confessional gives to the confessing secret teller "absolution." In the name and with the power of Jesus, the priest declares on behalf of the church that the person is forgiven. We Baptists and evangelical-type folks do a great job at pointing out sin and making people guilty. We make sin and secrets a real event. For us, sin is BIG. Yet at the same time we have a hard time making forgiveness of our secrets as big an event as our sins.

MAKING FORGIVENESS AN EVENT

A friend was preaching at a Baptist church in Florida that tries to make forgiveness as real as sin. They have a pond of water in the sanctuary. When they confess secrets to God, they throw a rock into the pond. They also have a shallow baking pan filled with sand at another place. They write their secrets and sins in the sand. Then, with a chopstick they cover them over with sand—gone forever. These folks are trying to make forgiving secrets as big an event as keeping them. Maybe you could come up with some ceremonies of your own.

A friend of mine tried to help his girlfriend stop smoking.

The doctors had already told her that she would die of emphysema if she did not stop. But none of these warnings worked. She even hid smoking from my friend. After work she would wash her hair and put on new clothes before they went to dinner. When my friend discovered her secret, they had a solemn ceremony on a bridge over the Trinity River in Fort Worth. Claiming 1 John 1:9 and the power of Christ, they hurled her cigarettes into the river. It was an act of forgiveness and freedom that was as big as the secret.

Authentic Christian friends hear your secrets and then bury them in the deep sea of God's own forgetfulness.

Confession has taken some weird turns in history. John of Kronstadt (1829-1908) was a charismatic Russian Orthodox priest. He had so many persons in his parish that he encouraged his parishioners to make their confessions together and out loud! That must have been some scene at church. Everyone was calling out their secrets out loud at the same time. The practice did not last after John died. But we can do better than that.

THE SEAL

Alongside the confessional in the ancient church, they also developed the "seal" of the confessional. The priest receiving the confession must not under any circumstances reveal the sins of the confessing Christians. The church took on this responsibility with enormous seriousness. The "seal" of the confessional guaranteed that the person telling his or her secrets would not be compromised by revelation of those secrets to anyone, ever.

Again, we should learn something from the ancient practice of the "seal." The wise man wrote, "Hatred stirs up strife, but love covers all sins" (Proverbs 10:12). When you know someone's secret, you keep it under cover. You do not expose it.

James was the younger half-brother of Jesus who grew up in the same Nazarene home. He was pastor of the church in Jerusalem and a Christian martyr. The last word to drip from his pen was a reminder about keeping secrets. When you hear someone's secret and help them turn away from it, you "cover a multitude of sins" (James 5:20). Authentic Christian friends hear your secrets and then bury them in the deep sea of God's own forgetfulness.

This also includes the way we publicly intercede for one another. Too often, Christian prayer groups become hotbeds of salacious gossip: "Lord, please help Esther Jones, since we found out her husband is sleeping with his secretary and they had an awful confrontation last week. Lord, help Esther wisely use the money she took from their joint account to hire a divorce lawyer. Lord, give her wisdom." Unfortunately, we have been in prayer meetings like that where prayer is used as a device to reveal someone's deepest secrets. Put a cork in it! God put two guards in front of your tongue—lips and teeth. Use them to clam up.

One of mankind's greatest books, *Confessions*, by Augustine of Hippo Regius in Africa (St. Augustine), involved Augustine telling his secrets to all the ages. In addition, the German Romantic poet, Goethe, considered everything he wrote to be one great confession.

Now, for a Baptist like me, all of this church history is pretty heavy. I have deep respect for my Catholic friends and have learned from them about the power of confession. Some of us, however, believe that all believers are priests. Peter himself addressed all Christians as

> *Not everyone can handle your secret, so not everyone should hear your secret.*

a "holy priesthood" (1 Peter 2:5). The late Carlyle Marney, a Baptist preacher from my hometown of Austin, Texas, wrote a book called *Priests to One Another*. He said that if every believer is a priest, then every believer has the right to hear the secrets of another Christian and accept the responsibility to keep those secrets secret. But what does this mean to the one telling the secret and the one hearing the secret?

In just that regard, I have written a number of very personal things in this book concerning my wife's family and my sons. I have the explicit permission to tell these stories from all of them. You cannot reveal the secrets of other people without their very clear permission to do so.

WHO SHOULD HEAR YOUR SECRET?

This may be one of the hardest things you ever decide. Not everyone can handle your secret, so not everyone should hear your secret. In every church and community, there are those souls who are marked out for wisdom, discretion, and prudence. That is, they have a solid track record. If you stop right now, you can think of individuals like that. People turn to them for advice. They are not gossips. They listen more than they speak. They are never quick to judge any situation. People gravitate to them when they have problems.

Do not blurt it out in one paragraph at Starbucks while people are ordering triple-grande skinny lattes three feet from you.

In fact, such people are known to be good keepers of secrets. They never talk about other people in a negative light. They look for the best in others. They actually try to cover up the mistakes of others in a good sort of way. These keepers of secrets never use people's stuff against them. They do not go around town saying, "Gotcha." This is the kind of person you may approach with your secret.

A pastor was retiring after forty years in the same church. At his retirement dinner he joked, "You had better hope I never lose my mind and start talking. What I know about some of you would not do to tell." Some of us in the ministry will go to the grave with thousands of other people's secrets. Pray we do not lose our mind in the extended care center!

When you approach such a trusted person, first say that you want to tell them something personal. Suggest that you would like to share something with them that you need to tell someone. Then stop. Look at them and then listen to their response. They will telegraph to you through what they say or do not say that they are willing to hear your secret. Ask God for wisdom.

> *But real cleansing and emancipation comes when you take responsibility for your part in the secret.*

You may find a place to tell your hurts, habits, and hangups in meetings such as Celebrate Recovery, made famous by Pastor Rick Warren. Others find Alcoholics Anonymous a safe and secure setting. This international organization has a stellar record of group confession. Other persons have put together their own confessional and accountability groups.

HOW SHOULD YOU TELL YOUR SECRET?

First, be sure there is a safe place and plenty of time. Do not blurt it out in one paragraph at Starbucks while people are ordering triple-grande skinny lattes three feet from you. Instead, take time to give the whole story in a private setting. Also, give a context to the secret. Emptying your heart requires a narrative, so tell the story from beginning to end.

Be careful that you do not make yourself the hero of the story and everyone else the villains. You have to own who you are before you can disown who you are. Some folks like to tell their secrets in a way that makes them the victim. Tell the truth about yourself. For example, if you have not had sex with your husband for three years and he has committed adultery, you need to tell both sides of that story. If you were part of the problem that caused the secret, own it when you tell it. It is a temptation to tell part of the secret and hide part of it. But real cleansing and emancipation comes when you take responsibility for your part in the secret.

On the other hand, do not take yourself too seriously. Some sensitive folks take their secret so seriously that they refuse to accept the relief that comes from telling it. They go from friend to friend, counselor to counselor, pastor to pastor and tell the same thing over and over. Martin Luther did this to his own confessor. Finally, the confessor got mad and told Martin, "Stop! Come back when you have some real sins to confess." Some poor souls are overly scrupulous. Make your confession like Nike's motto—just do it. When it is done, accept the grace of God and go on.

Have confidence that when you tell your secret, you can have relief. God is faithful. Stuart Hamblen became one of American's first singing cowboys in 1926. He went on to become a singer,

actor, radio host and songwriter. He wrote this song years ago
when he came to Christ at a Billy Graham crusade:

> The chimes of time ring out the news
> Another day is through
> Someone slipped and fell
> Was that someone you?
>
> You may have longed for added strength
> Your courage to renew
> Do not be disheartened
> For I have news for you
>
> It is no secret what God can do,
> What He's done for others, He'll do for you.
> With arms wide open, He'll pardon you.
> It is no secret what God can do.
>
> There is no night; for in His light
> You never walk alone
> Always feel at home
> Wherever you may go
>
> There is no power can conquer you
> While God is on your side
> Take Him at His promise
> Don't run and hide

It is no secret what God can do
What He's done for others, He'll do for you
With arms wide open He'll pardon you
It is no secret what God can do.

SEARCHING THROUGH OUR SECRETS

1. Have you ever experienced God's grace in confession in such a way that His forgiveness is as big an event as your sin?

2. Who would you confess to with confidence? What would be the setting where you would do so?

3. How could evangelical Christians find more ways to make confession possible, confidential, and accessible? How could that happen in creative ways in your church?

4. Do you ask the permission of those among your family and friends before you tell their secrets to others?

5. Do you actually believe in the biblical promises of the forgiveness of God—that He buries your sins in the deepest sea and puts them behind His back and remembers them no more?

6. How could you convince someone hiding a secret that God will indeed forgive them? Could you invent a ceremony (like throwing the cigarettes in the river) that would mark the moment and make forgiveness as big an event as sin?

NO MORE
SECRETS

"*Hell is truth seen too late.*"

-THOMAS HOBBES

CHAPTER 7

TIMING

To everything there is a season,
A time for every purpose under heaven...
A time to keep silence,
And a time to speak....

(ECCLESIASTES 3:1,7)

The wise old Jewish sage who wrote these words had experienced everything a person can experience. Among other things, he had developed a strong sense of the right time to say something and when not to do so.

You have been reading this book. Perhaps you are gripped by a growing urgency to tell your secret to someone. Each chapter of this book has made that urgency loom larger. It is time to think about timing. Not every moment is opportune to tell your secret. Instead, you need to find God's timing.

Carl Jung, the theistic founder of psychoanalysis, placed great emphasis on timing. In fact, he invented a sixty-four dollar word for a certain kind of time: *synchronicity.* (Now, don't get me wrong.

I am not a scholar. I did major in Greek at Baylor University and took all I could get at Southwestern, not always because I wanted to but because I needed to.) Anyway, that word consists of a preposition, *soon,* and a noun for time, *chronos.* Synchronicity points to those things that happen with time, at just the right time. Jung made a careful study of this critical reality of life.

WHEN THINGS BUG YOU

Jung had a patient who was locked down in life. She could not respond to anything and had turned inward and withdrawn. This was due to secrets in her life. Try as he would, Jung could not help. Then, one night she dreamed of a giant scarab beetle, a big, old, ugly bug. (That would not be my favorite dream.) She had an appointment to consult again with Jung the next day. Sitting in his consultation room with her back to a large window, she began to tell Jung about her dream. While they were talking, something started to hit the window, again and again. With her back to the window she could not see it. Jung was facing her and the window, so he could see it.

It was a giant scarab beetle banging against the window pane. Jung opened the window, grabbed it with his hand, and showed it to her. It caught her attention, for sure. (That would have scared the living daylights out of yours truly!) She had dreamed about that bug, was telling him about that bug, and that bug was trying to get into the window. When he showed her the bug, the timing of it unleashed the secrets that had held her back in life and health. Jung used that story to illustrate synchronicity. The preacher in me would call that divine timing.

IT'S A GOD THING

We have all had moments similar to that. Things just fall together in a way you could never explain other than by an act of God. You are thinking about an old friend you have not seen for years when suddenly he calls you. You are trying to remember something you read, and you wish you could remember where you read it. You pick up a book, and it falls open to that very place. We call those events "God moments."

Often, when it is time to tell your secret, a God moment happens. The right person at the right time is in

Often, when it is time to tell your secret, a God moment happens.

the right place, and then you can tell your secret. I am sharing things in this book because it is the right time to share them. A while back, it would have been too early. The stories were too much, the topic was too hot, the outcome was too recent, and it would have been awkward. On the other hand, it is time to share these principles with you now. I could not wait five years more to write this book. This is God's timing.

HOW YOU RECOGNIZE GOD'S TIMING

Jesus lived with a sense of God's timing. He saw a clock no one else could see and watched a calendar invisible to everyone else. Once, He even told his mother, "My hour has not yet come" (John 2:4). It was not time to tell His secret about who He was. Later, however, He would clearly say that His hour had come.

God has a way of marking the moment when you should tell.

The Gospel of Mark deals with His "messianic secret." Over and over He told folks not to tell anyone what He had done for them (Mark 1:44). He did not want to tell His secret prematurely. If Jesus waited for the right time to tell His secret, so should you. Not every moment is equal when telling your secret.

When it is time to tell your secret, you will have a sense of certainty and peace. That does not mean it will be easy. It does mean that your inward self will have a sense that this is the right time. You may be nervous, even reluctant. Yet deep within, you will know it is time to tell.

When it is time to tell your secret, God's timing will put the right person in front of you at the right time. A friend of mine in the ministry was dealing secretly with a situation that could have destroyed him and his ministry. He urgently needed to tell his secret. At an appointment with one of his best friends in the ministry, that caring friend asked the question: "What is the

worst thing I could know about you?" My friend did not expect
that question. It came out of the blue. Yet it demonstrated that
very moment was the time and place to tell his secret. That
secret revealed at that time helped save his life and ministry.
God has a way of marking the moment when you should tell.

THE RIGHT TIME:
A DIVINE PRE-ARRANGEMENT

The Bible is chock-full of stories about the right time. In Acts
8, an Ethiopian had been to Jerusalem and was now going home
to Africa. He was a eunuch. Bottom line, he had been castrated.
Sometimes the royal families would do that to men who worked
around the harem to ward off trouble. Yet there was a law against
someone who had been mutilated going into the temple at
Jerusalem. It may be that he had turned back when he heard of
that prohibition. Maybe he went in despite his secret. For whatever reason, he was going home pondering a biblical passage.

God had told the deacon Philip to go to a desert road.
(I had a few deacons that I would have liked to send down a
desert road, but that is another story.) Philip was hitchhiking in
the middle of nowhere. God told Philip to put his thumb out
and chase down the eunuch's chariot. Hearing the eunuch
reading from Isaiah, he jumped into the passenger seat. In a few
minutes Philip explained that the text was about Jesus,

written seven hundred years before He came to earth.

The Ethiopian had been hindered in Jerusalem, but his entire life had been a hindrance. He asked Philip, "What hinders me from being baptized?" (v. 36). Philip met him at the point of his secret and baptized him then and there in a creek in the desert. All of that was a matter of the right person and the right time and the right place. It was a God thing.

My dad's life verse was Proverbs 3:6: "In all thy ways acknowledge Him and He will direct your paths." Live in a sensitive relationship to God's timing, and He will show you when to share your secret or when to be ready to hear the secret of another. He is the God of *all* times—and the God of *your* time.

YOUR TIME

It may just be that your picking up this book is just because this is your time. It is no accident. Your disappointment may be His appointment with you. A cruel atheist wrote on a marker board in front of some challenged little children: GOD IS NOWHERE. One of the most desperate cases took an eraser, entered one space between two letters, and wrote, GOD IS NOW HERE. Sometimes all you need is a little space.

Yet when you tell someone your secret, you need to take care. Some people simply cannot help but talk. You can identify them easily. When they are with you, they talk about everyone except you. Rest assured that they will tell your secrets as well. Seek out quiet people, listening people, prudent people—those people others trust. You can figure out who they are.

Yet it is likely that you can find someone to share your secret with who will also need to tell you their secret. This is the "Boomerang Principle." You know what a boomerang is. Australians throw them at stuff, and they come back to the thrower. In the Scriptures that is called the "one another" effect, or a reciprocal effect. We are exhorted to love one another, carry one another's burdens, forgive one another, and confess our sins to one another (James 6:5).

You don't have to be in Australia to use a boomerang.

SEARCHING THROUGH OUR SECRETS

1. Can you recall an occasion when timing in conversation made all the difference in the outcome?
2. In what kind of conversation is timing the most significant, and how do you estimate that?
3. Have you had any reports of mistimed conversations recently? What would have been the difference in impact?
4. Can you wait too long to have a conversation?
5. What are some evidences from the life of the Lord Jesus that He had a perfect sense of timing?

NO MORE
SECRETS

"*It is wise not to seek a secret
and honest not to reveal one.*"

-William Penn

Chapter Eight
....

Mending Broken People

It is a memorable moment in a remarkable movie, *The Fugitive*. U. S. marshal Sam Gerard (Tommy Lee Jones) is chasing Dr. Richard Kimble (Harrison Ford). Kimble has run to the end of a gigantic drainage pipe and has to jump into the water in the end in order to get away from Gerard. Kimble cries out from one end of the pipe to Gerard at the other: "I didn't do it." Gerard calls out to Kimble: "I don't care."

Kimble jumps and Gerard keeps chasing him. Gerard meant that he could not care less about the guilt or innocence of Kimble. He had a job to do: catch Kimble.

This suggests another scenario. What if someone is chasing you and you really DID do it? Even worse, what if someone catches you in the very act? Your secret is no longer a secret. You experience a "gotcha" moment. You are discovered, outed, and exposed. You were caught in the act, whatever the act is.

But flip that script. What if you are the catcher? Suppose you run into somebody somewhere doing something he should not be doing—whatever. It could be a deacon gambling at a casino fifteen hundred miles away from home or a Sunday school teacher lurching out of a bar at 2 a.m. with a strange companion, you name it. You nail them. You catch them in the very moment, face to face and toe to toe. There is no denying it. They are busted.

What is your attitude and your response going to be? Will you look the other way, whistle in the dark, and act like you are both invisible? Will you sneer at them and make a snarky remark? Will you confront them like a street preacher and scream, "Repent! Turn or burn!"? Or will you do something else, suggested in the apostle Paul's letter to the church in Galatia (modern-day Turkey)?

SIT ON THE BARREL

In Galatians 6, Paul presents a realistic scenario. One Christian observes another overtaken in a "fault." Now, to be clear, this is not some snoopy sister out cruising the town looking for dirt on a church member. This is not some brother Pharisee trying to spy on a friend who is the object of gossip. We are not talking about private detective action here. That is beneath the Christian life. We are not the Christian CIA or the disciples' Gestapo trying to catch one another sinning. Indeed, Christian love means we think the best of one another, not the worst.

There was a young monk who was a novice in an ancient monastery. During the novitiate, a young monk spends years discerning whether or not he has the gift to take the vows of poverty, chastity, and obedience for the rest of his life. He would live and die at the monastery. He would never have his own money or touch a woman, and must obey the abbot for the rest of his life. This particular young monk had smuggled a woman into his cell. Suspicious about his behavior, the other monks informed the abbot. The abbot went with them to surprise the young monk in his cell.

When the young monk heard the posse coming down the hall of the monastery, he made the girl get into a barrel in the corner of his room. The wise old abbot knocked on the door with the suspicious monks. He instantly discerned what was happening: the girl was in the barrel. The old abbot went and sat on the barrel and told the other monks to search the room. They looked above, under, and behind everything. Then the abbot chastised the surprised, suspicious brothers: "How dare you accuse this fine young novice of having a secret woman in his cell? Get out of here."

When the older monks slinked out one by one, the abbot was left alone in the cell with the novice. He got off the barrel and looked the novice in the eyes. The novice knew that the old abbot intuited exactly what had happened and who was in the barrel. The abbot did not open the barrel. He simply said, "Go and sin no more." The young monk never sinned in this area again. The old abbot's gentle protection and great grace converted him to a life of genuine piety.

It is always the right Christian attitude to sit on the barrel when you discover a fallen brother or sister.

No, this is not about someone who finds someone doing something they would rather not find them doing. That is not a "gotcha" moment but an "uh-oh" moment that you would rather not be having. You have stumbled on an erring brother or sister. Keep in mind this particular scenario only involves the church family. Paul is writing about an event that is all in the family, in the household of faith.

When you stumble on an unbelieving friend or co-worker doing something you think they should not be doing, that is another matter. Christians need to settle something once and for all: LOST PEOPLE ACT LOST. We are not supposed to condemn lost people to their face when we discover them sinning in secret. They cannot help what they are doing because they are prisoners of sin. Instead, you point lost people to CHRIST. Evangelical Christians in America have done a good job of alienating our mission field by pointing fingers in judgment.

MENDING NETS AND SETTING BONES

What do you do when you catch a friend who has fallen into sin? Paul uses a fascinating word in the language of his day that refers to mending nets or setting a broken bone. Both metaphors reveal much. Let me try to unpack a little of it.

Paul uses the same word as the one in Mark 1:19, when James and John were sitting in their father Zebedee's boat mending the fishing nets. Now, it was a routine matter for fishing nets to get torn. They snag on rocks, get caught up in stuff in the sea, get old, and wear out. It just happens. But you do not throw the whole net away because it ripped in one place. Instead, you mend the net.

Now, I have never mended a net, but I can imagine what it's like in comparison to another fishing problem. A long time ago, before I could go to Cabela's or Bass Pro Shops and buy fancy fishing reels that never backlash, I had to fish with an open-faced reel. When I cast the reel, the line would hit the top of the water and stop on the spot because there was nowhere for more line to go. But here was the problem: The reel kept on spinning and created something called "backlash." The line wound around itself in the reel, tangled, knotted up, laced together, and messed up. It seemed to take forever to straighten out our backlash of little loops and line circled around line—a mare's nest of fishing line. It took time and patience to straighten out backlash. You old-timers know what I'm writing about.

I can imagine that is what it's like to repair a net. It takes patience, understanding, endurance, and the will to keep on at the task. When you find a brother or sister in a fault, all of those qualities must be present in your attitude toward him or her. You cannot mend a net quickly, nor can you fix a broken Christian with one latte at Starbucks. It takes time. Mending a net takes patience, and so does mending Christians. Most Christians caught in the act are either defensive or mad to begin with. They rationalize, they point at other hypocrites, and they may even point at your own failings.

Indeed, restoration work is slow work. You have to work on some folks one inch at a time to get them back to where they need to be.

I have a very good friend who is a minister. Oftentimes, his friends point out his past failings in order to excuse their own! As much as anything else, restoring a wayward brother or sister takes an act of will. Down inside the parliament of your personality and the congress of your conscious, you have the will to restore someone. Most church folks, unfortunately, do not want to mess with fallen Christians. Instead, they play the quiet game and look the other way. They smile at the broken Christian and walk right on by like the priest and Levite who left the broken man in the ditch. Unfortunately, there are not many Good Samaritans out there.

Restoration is also like setting a broken bone. Last time I broke a bone, I did not want to see the orthopedic surgeon coming at me with a chain saw. Setting a broken bone takes sensitivity, tact, knowledge, a light touch, and the patience to do it slowly and in the right way. If you mishandle a broken bone, you can make it worse. When you find a broken Christian, you must not wallop them with a family Bible and throw an offering plate at them like a Frisbee. Instead, care, concern, prayer, and gentleness are in order.

Penin Brambilla Barcilon took twenty years to restore Leonardo's masterpiece, *The Last Supper*. It hangs in the remains of a monastery dining room in Milan, Italy. Over the centuries that immortal painting had been destroyed inch by inch. The crazy monks had cut out a door in the bottom of the painting where Jesus' feet are in order to get into their kitchen. They burned lamps and candles that covered the glowing colors with centuries of soot. Then the Allies bombed Milan during World War II and destroyed everything but the painting. Barcilon took two decades to restore the fresco. She had to work one inch at a time to remove the grime of the centuries and the smoke from the fires. Now you can see the original colors. Indeed, restoration work is slow work. You have to work on some folks one inch at a time to get them back to where they need to be.

MEEK IS NOT WEAK

Paul adds another word of caution in this verse. Our mending and knitting together of a broken Christian must not be done in a spirit of superiority or condescending egotism. Rather, we must restore another person in a spirit of meekness. This is the attitude that Jesus blessed in His beatitudes. He even called Himself "meek and lowly." We might want to look at how He restored a couple of folks.

The eighth chapter of John tells the story of a woman taken in the very act of adultery. Someone came into the tent or the room and found her in the act with a man who was not her husband. You can imagine the searing sun scalding her eyes as they dragged her out of the dark room. The passion turned to terror in a few seconds. She was thrown out into the dust of the street by a group of angry men. Frankly, it looked like the scenes you see of radical Islamic stoning today. (Of course, the guy got away.) There she is, in the street surrounded by men with stones in their hands, ready to crush her skull. She would close her eyes on earth for the last time as a barrage of rocks cracked her head open.

Then, along came Jesus. He turned the attention away from her and instead focused on the heart of every man there. He invited the sinless man to cast the first stone. One by one, they dropped their stones and left the scene. Then Jesus stooped down to look straight into her eyes. He told her that He did not condemn her either. The well-known story mentions that He wrote something in the sand. Scholars down through the ages have wondered what he wrote. Perhaps it was the names of the very men in that crowd who had slept with her. Or maybe it was an intimate personal message that only she would understand. At any rate, it was a healing message. It might have been the ancient equivalent of a modern Valentine heart. Or maybe Jesus was just doodling in the dirt to give her time to compose herself and quietly leave. He just gave her space. In other words, He sat on the barrel.

Whatever the message in the sand was, it was the picture of a gentle, personal, risky, and patient restoration job. As another example, consider Jesus' restoration of Peter after Rocky denied Him three times, once with a screaming "#*@%* it, I don't know Him." That is what an "oath" means. We preachers pretty it up in the pulpit so we don't scare the WMU. But Peter actually used a curse word in his denial.

Paul warns those in restoration projects to watch themselves because restoration, in some strange way, may lead them into temptation as well.

In John 21 Jesus encountered Peter at dawn on the Sea of Galilee. He had fished all night and caught nothing. Jesus ordered Pete to throw the net on the other side, and he caught 153 fish. Peter knew who the stranger was then, so he quickly waded to shore. Jesus was there in that fish camp on that frosty morning. The smell of roasted fish was in the air, and Jesus gave Peter some fish and bread.

Jesus did not say, "You disappointing coward, you pitiful ingrate, you total failure. I knew you did not have what it takes." No. Jesus asked Peter three times, "Do you love Me?" When Peter told Jesus how much he loved Him, the Lord simply told

Peter, "Feed My sheep." That was all—words of love and confidence. Not a gotcha to be heard. You could hear the gentle lapping of the waves on the sand of the shore. Pentecost was in that moment.

CONSIDER YOURSELF

There is a mysterious relationship between restoring someone else and your own temptation. Paul warns those in restoration projects to watch themselves because restoration, in some strange way, may lead them into temptation as well. If you get too close to the fire, you can get burnt. Helping someone else out of a secret may tempt you to keep a dark secret. It is a mystery, but it is also the truth. When you know the weakness of someone you thought to be strong, you may use it as an excuse to rationalize your own weakness.

While you are restoring someone else, don't turn into a project yourself!

SEARCHING THROUGH OUR SECRETS

1. When have you kept another person's secret? How candid did they feel, and how did you feel?
2. When has someone kept your secret? How did

you feel about that, and how did it affect your relationship?

3. Can you remember a time you actively participated in mending a broken Christian friend? Or, can you recall a time that your church did so?

4. What is the dynamic in Paul's warning to take care in restoring someone else that you not be tempted in the same way? Can you recall an incident in which a mending person also fell into this temptation?

5. Should you seek to mend someone who does not want to be mended?

"You don't choose your family.
They are God's gift to you
as you are to them."

-DESMOND TUTU

CHAPTER 9

IN MY OWN BACKYARD: DUSTY'S STORY

I am Dennis Swanberg. I have experienced a wonderful life of ministry. Yet I understand exactly what Paul meant when he called himself the "chief of sinners." I have experienced the light and privilege of Christian mentors, educators, leaders, and icons. Nevertheless, all of that light makes my own darkness even darker.

When reading Christ's Sermon on the Mount, one learns that the thought life is the hidden source of our acts. Although the consequences of lust and hate in the heart may not be adultery or murder, Christ considers the thought as if it is the deed.

My friend Steve Arterburn wrote an insightful and honest book entitled *Every Man's Battle*. As a man, I deal with everything Steve discusses in that book. I live on the road in hotels and airports, on planes and in rented cars. Every hallway, room, hotel restaurant, and lobby, along with related stores and malls, are replete with every temptation a man faces. It is by the grace of God that grace alone has kept me in its grip.

The most famous professor in the 108-year history of Southwestern Baptist Theological Seminary is Dr. "Cactus" Jack MacGorman. Vivid is the memory of that classroom icon when he told my class, "We must put on the boxing gloves every day." I recall right now thinking to myself, *If that old prof has to do that, how much more do I?* (Strange to think, I am now about the age he was when he said that in the '70s of the last century.) Yet I know now he was absolutely right.

Every day is a battle for every man and I expect for every woman in the same or other ways. Every day we battle with the world, the flesh, and the Devil. I must fight the good fight. Hypocrisy is not an option for any Christian, but most especially not for any minister, even though it is always easier to be the first to cast the stone at someone else. That is why I want to tell you our family story.

MY BOYS . . . RECOVERING ALCOHOLICS. HOW COULD THIS HAPPEN?

That is not an easy question to ask and even harder to answer. Wrestling with that answer in this book helps me, and I hope it will also help you. To help you understand how I tried to answer that hard question, I need to open up the secrets of my own family with their encouragement and permission.

My son Dustin had his first drink when he was twelve years old. In a strange way, it happened because of my own convictions. At a wedding ceremony, the couple I married was supposed to have non-alcoholic champagne. Like true Baptists, everybody was supposed to drink that at the reception and then hit the real stuff when they got in the privacy of their own homes. As it happened, however, the champagne was real. When the teetotalers recognized that the stuff was real alcohol, they left their full glasses on the reception tables, some more reluctantly than others.

After a good high school football game where he made a couple of tackles and a sack, he sneaked a six-pack out of the club, put on some good ol' George Jones, and emptied all six bottles by himself.

Wanting to be the center of attention, though, Dustin went around chugging down the full glasses. So he tasted his first alcohol at the age of twelve.

Dustin went to a Christian school and I was a pastor, so our lives were always under inspection. At sixteen years of age, Dustin hung around the country club golf course and knew how to get into the club kitchen undetected. After a good high school football game where he made a couple of tackles and a sack, he sneaked a six-pack out of the club, put on some good ol' George Jones, and emptied all six bottles by himself. This might have given us all a clue had we known it. Alcoholism ran in my wife's family, so the addiction gene was always lurking. Yet Dustin did not drink excessively in high school for fear of being caught by his coaches.

A PROFESSIONAL DRINKER IN COLLEGE

Like thousands of Christian kids in the South, the road to college became the road for a different lifestyle. Away from Mom and Dad in a new environment, and feeling like a man for the first time, Dustin jumped the tracks into a new relationship with alcohol. Thursday nights were the time to party since the joints had two-for-one pitchers. Yet Dustin was also on the way to a secret life. He recognized that with social media, Facebook, and all the rest, he could not hide his drinking. That led to his fateful decision to become a secret drinker, a professional at planning and hiding what he was doing—a subconscious slave in the addiction army, under King Alcohol.

Dustin devised a secret plan. One rainy Saturday morning (and he loves rainy days), he went to a mini-mart and bought two 24-ounce bottles of beer. Because he did not want to be discovered drinking in the dorm or on campus, he headed to a distant subdivision where the speed limit was 25 miles per hour. Alone, where his friends would not see him, he put on his country favorites and chugged down both bottles. Then he threw them in the gutter so there would be no evidence in his car.

When he got back to his room he sensed calm, a strange sense of well-being. The "magic" happened as he experienced the artificial sense of peace and serenity from alcohol. He had long suffered from ADHD, and the beers calmed the static in his head. The discontent, restlessness, and distraction were gone. He discovered how to drink just enough to reach this state of neutrality. Dustin felt normal when he drank—the false promise that alcohol has provided to millions of men and women.

Dustin felt normal when he drank—the false promise that alcohol has provided to millions of men and women.

He then locked in this pattern of behavior: heading out in the early morning to the mini-mart, going for the musical drive around the subdivision, ditching the evidence, and then returning to the dorm, chilled out for another day. On the days he did not do this, the static returned and the restlessness reigned.

Then Dustin had his first public disaster. As a junior in college in 2007, he went with his buddies to a bar. There was great music, and one drink led to another one. A friend tried to pocket his keys, but he decided to drive back to campus. He made his grand entry by TAKING OUT A STOP SIGN, hitting three cars, and smashing into a tree. With his alcohol-addled brain he decided he would avoid detection if he went into the dorm, put on his pajamas, and went straight to bed.

He discovered that night the self-deception that goes with addiction. At 2:15 a.m. the police showed up and the dorms emptied. Kids in their pajamas and robes were gawking at his wrecked car as he was hauled off to jail for twenty-four hours. He was a campus leader, a BMOC, but now he was in jail. He was so ashamed, he could not even pick up the Gideon Bible in his cell. His brother showed up and bailed him out. The cat was now out of the bag.

SOBER FOR TWO WEEKS, THEN A DOWNHILL SLIDE

Dusty got a "get out of jail" card. We took his car away for two months. Folks were understanding, and friends and family alike cut him some slack. After appearing before the board of the college, he did some community service. (He lived alone at this time.)

Our son was sober for the next two weeks. Then one night some of his buddies wanted him to go out for a steak, but he had another idea. Alone and without a car, he put on a hoodie and boots, and with cash in his pockets, tramped down the road on foot to a Mexican restaurant a mile away. The sight of the bright lights promised some relief for his restlessness and loneliness. He started out with his usual beers but then used them to chase shots of bourbon. He made a new friendly enemy—hard liquor. This started him down the road to a new level of professional alcoholism.

He eventually got his car back, resumed some of his collegiate activities—and made other plans as well. He devised a way to hide flasks in his boots so there was always a handy shot of bourbon. He plotted how to have secret stashes at convenient places. He fooled us and his friends—and even tried to fool God Himself. His days were planned around gaining access to alcohol. His last days at school were spent rooming with a family friend who was seldom there.

In the loneliness and isolation, his fear grew as he faced an unknown future. He was haunted by my own visibility and success and his brother's

Isn't that what a father is supposed to do, be the rescuer? Isn't that the way to "keep things quiet"?

expectations. He was afraid of leaving a lifestyle of drinking and being a "somebody" on his college campus and then entering the real world a "nobody." Dusty's only tool for coping with life was alcohol. What was next? The alcoholism tolerance grew deeper and wider as the college chapter of his life was coming to an end.

After graduation Dustin was in Fort Worth with the family on December 28th. He decided to go to Austin to visit other family members. Following his familiar routine, he loaded up his traveling music (he always had to have the right music to drink by!) and headed down I-35 to the capital of Texas. Of course, he sipped his bourbon on the way while imbibing some quart-sized beers, just enough to keep the buzz going while heading to meet his cousins for "movie night."

Late to the movie but feeling fine, he went the wrong way on a one-way access feeder road to the theater. Then came the flashing lights, the sirens, and another disaster. After a breathalyzer test, he went straight to jail. This time he was thrown into a drunk tank with forty-two characters of all sorts and backgrounds. His cousins, mother, brother, and I did not know where he

Yet he was still in denial and blamed the judicial system for his problems.

was. It occurred to Lauree and me to start calling jails. Our nieces helped out. One of them finally found him in Georgetown, Texas.

Chad and I jumped into the car and drove eight hours to the jailhouse. I was going to bail Dustin out. Isn't that what a father is supposed to do, be the rescuer? Isn't that the way to "keep things quiet"? But through a random phone call from a friend, it was as if God spoke audibly to me that early morning: "Leave him there." It was a revelation out of heaven. It was tight, but it was right. I obeyed the voice. At just the time Dusty thought he was going to be bailed out, the jailer asked him, "What size jump suit do you wear?" That is when Dustin knew this was sure enough for real. No bail, no rescue, and no more communication at that time. The jailer told Dustin, "No one is here for you."

The result was cold-turkey detox in the drunk tank. Dustin suffered chills, sweat, palpitations, shaking, shivering, and all of the demons that accompany instant detox without any palliative to relieve his situation. It did not help that some of the forty-two guys in the tank with him offered their sardonic encouragement: "We know what you are going through." Unable to eat properly for days, our youngest son lost thirteen pounds detoxing on a metal bed.

On the eighth day, Dusty called. We told him we would come to get him but would take him to an unidentified place. Yet he was still in denial and blamed the judicial system for his problems. On the ninth day, we showed up, picked him up, and took him directly to DFW and put him on a jet to California. A pilot friend of the family got Lauree and me through security so we could watch him directly as he boarded the plane. Lauree cried and I hurt as Dusty walked down the jet-way, looking back for a moment and then looking ahead with only a bag, a Bible, and a rock-bottom experience that was the genesis of a journey into a new reality.

LONG NIGHT'S JOURNEY INTO DAY

Arriving at the treatment center in San Clemente, California, he was still in denial. For the first three days, Dusty considered all of the other patients to be the ones with a problem. As the son of Dennis Swanberg, he could handle everything himself. In his mind, he was just the victim of bad luck, ADHD, and a broken judicial system. On the fourth day, a group of the patients took the "druggie buggy" to the beach. Sitting on the sand with the Pacific waves lapping at the west end of the USA, Dusty, like the prodigal son in Luke 15, came to himself. Like him, Dustin had spent years trying to be more than he was supposed to be and then years being less than he was meant to be. By the ocean that day, he came to be the Dustin he was meant to be. For the first time, Dustin admitted that he had a problem, he was powerless, and he needed help.

> *Dustin had spent years trying to be more than he was supposed to be and then years being less than he was meant to be.*

The future unfolded in rapid and positive succession. I got Dusty a place to live with friends in Tennessee. He lived in a small room, took their kids to school, became a telemarketer for a publishing company, worked his way through the Twelve Steps of AA, and faced the future. After eighteen months, he moved to Mansfield, Texas, to be a summer youth intern at a friend's church. Then it was back to Tennessee and on to Pennsylvania where Dusty gave his testimony, only to find out how many men were hurting in the same way.

This opened up his future as a ministry for those with similar problems. Dustin enrolled in Southwestern, my old seminary, and then later transferred to New Orleans Baptist Seminary for additional studies. He's had a multitude of church positions and is now working in the secular marketplace. He has found a real sense of peace and tranquility by continuing to help others through various recovery ministries and programs in north central Texas.

In August 2015, Dustin walked down the aisle with his brother by his side. This time it wasn't down the aisle of a jailhouse, or in a courtroom, but in a beautiful chapel at sunset to stand by his bride, Britny. He was ready to begin a new life together with someone who understood him for who he was, loved him in spite of his failures, and promised to believe the past does not decide the future.

> *Yet he has learned an abiding truth: "Never doubt in the dark what God has showed you in the light."*

Fast forward, and their marriage is Christ centered and growing stronger each day. When I asked Dustin to read how I wrote his story and give his permission to share it with you, he gladly agreed. He will be the first to tell you that the struggle is real, every day. Dustin will always wrestle with the temptation that ensnared him to begin with. Yet he has learned an abiding truth: "Never doubt in the dark what God has showed you in the light."

He wanted to leave you with one of his favorite quotes from

a man he admires very much. Dr. John Hagee has been a friend to Dustin and our family for years.

He carries this with him daily . . . .

> "Sometimes you have to let go of the life you pictured, in order to have the life that God has planned."

LESSONS LEARNED IN THE LABORATORY OF LIFE

Life is lived forward but understood backward. Looking in the rearview mirror, I have realized some truths from our family story that might help the reader.

1. *You can be living in the middle of a secret and not even know it.* Lauree and I were unaware of what was happening in Dustin's life. We sometimes had a vague sense that all was not well, but we could not put our finger on it. Moreover, Chad was enabling his brother's behavior while wrestling with the same problem himself. He could not blow the whistle on Dustin without risking our awareness of his own problems. Secrets happen, and you do not know it. Perhaps that should not surprise any family.

2. *Most things come to light.* Even as a "professional

alcoholic," Dustin finally ran out of schemes. You can be a chameleon for only so long before you wear yourself out changing colors to match your environment. Just like Edgar Allan Poe's story, "Tell-Tale Heart," you reveal yourself even when you do not wish to do so. Most of us spend our lives pretending that everyone else is found out, but we will not be. However, that is usually not the case.

3. *Enablers have to stop enabling.* I take my share of responsibility for being an enabler, sometimes knowing it and sometimes being ignorant of it. The hardest thing I have done in my life was to leave Dustin in that jail in Georgetown. Yet all of the positive and redemptive things that happened after that were wrapped up in that moment of truth.

4. *God is already putting people in your future that you do not even know will be there.* The folks in California and the Begin Recovery Project were waiting in the wings for just the right moment to come into our story. You will be surprised who is ready to help.

5. *The best folks to help other folks are those who sat where they sit.* Dustin now has a ministry based on 2 Corinthians 1:4 (NLT), "He comforts us in

all our troubles so that we can comfort others. When they are troubled, we will be able to give them the same comfort God has given us." Dustin sat where they sit. No one can help someone like another person who has been there but found the way out.

6. *God can recycle the strangest junk and use it for his purposes.* On the Caribbean island of St. Lucia, there is a "Beer Bottle Church." The local beer bottles are deep seafoam-green. The church members took the bottles and mortared them together to make the walls of a church. The sunlight coming through the green of the bottles makes you feel that you are in the ocean looking at a beautiful color. God did a similar thing by recycling Dustin's pain into His providence.

SEARCHING THROUGH OUR SECRETS

1. What might be the possible signs that a friend or family member is hiding behaviors that are self-destructive?

2. If you were confronted with the same decision Dennis confronted—to leave Dustin in jail or to bail him out—what elements would you weigh?

3. How can we as individuals weigh secret habits in

our own lives? How do we move into reality concerning the toxic nature of our own secret lives?

4. What are the signs of enabling the undermining activities or those close to us?

5. Imagine other outcomes for this episode. Simon Wiesenthal, in his famous story, "Sunflower," had a number of persons write alternative endings. What could be other endings for this story?

6. Is there any action prompted by this story that you should take right now? How will you take it?

NO MORE SECRETS

"People are secretive

when they have secrets."

-DEB CASTELLI

Chapter Ten

It's All in the Family

TRUTHFINDER.COM

There is a search engine with the URL called TruthFinder. com. It sends unsolicited advertisements to me, so I have no hesitation about revealing its existence. To use it, you type in someone's name and presto . . . you find out everything about them in public records: addresses, arrests, tickets, and much more. Some claim that the site is addictive because you just cannot stop poking around into individuals' pasts.

An interesting thought came to me: What if you could type in a family name into a TruthFinder.com on steroids and find out every secret in the life of every family you know? You could type in the names of folks with known challenges as well as of those with "perfect families." You could ask about the real scoop on the marital life of your friends, and the real poop on the failures of their children. Of course, no such site exists.

Yet the Bible itself provides a sort of TruthFinder.com with reference to the family lives of its heroes. We have already looked at Adam and Eve. The story of their sons, which belongs to the ages, ended with fratricide. And this was not just any murder, but rather the murder of one brother by another because of the outcome of a worship service! What a beginning to the human story.

> *How many times have you read a Bible story and wanted to ask God, "Why did you put up with these people?"*

The Bible presents human families—warts and all. That is one reason I believe in its truth and inspiration by God. No one would want to invent the stories in the Bible and lay them at the feet of the Creator God. How many times have you read a Bible story and wanted to ask God, "Why did you put up with these people?" Former Baylor president David E. Garland and his late wife Diana wrote a most revealing book entitled *Flawed Families of the Bible: How God's Grace Works through Imperfect Relationships.*[6] This remarkable book discloses the amazing stories of dysfunctional families in the Bible and the ways God used their secrets mixed with His grace to move His purposes forward.

Consider Abraham, the father of three great monotheistic religions. He lied about his wife, slept with her maid, and sent that maid off to the desert without enough food and water to keep her and his own son alive. But that is just the

---

6 David E. Garland and Diana A. Garland, *Flawed Families of the Bible: How God's Grace Works through Imperfect Relationships* (Grand Rapids, MI: Baker, 2007).

beginning. Jacob deceived his blind father, stole the birthright and blessings from his brother, tricked his brother-in-law, and played favorites with his own son Joseph. Moses tried to pull off an exodus by killing an Egyptian, and then he had to leave town. Gideon had seventy sons with his wives and another son, Abimelech, with his concubine—as if all those wives could not keep him satisfied. Abimelech killed all seventy of his half-brothers. King David killed a man to get his wife for himself. His son, Solomon, had a harem larger than the population of Match.com. These sordid stories are only a sample of the secrets in the Bible.

WHAT KIND OF SECRETS DO FAMILIES KEEP?

Most secrets have to do with sex, money, or power. These are the unending sources of conflicts in human life. Behind all of these is the face of pride. And behind pride is idolatry—putting someone or something in the place of God.

It is likely that the deepest secrets people keep may be in the realm of sex and intimate relationships. That kind of secrecy is far less evident outside the church, in secular society, than it is in church because the secular world no longer has shame. A recent article about teenage girls and their online sexual escapades explores a teen culture that has lost any sense of shame at all. This article shows us that teenage sex lives are just the reverse of secret lifestyles. Everything is online for all to see.[7] The theme of the total loss of any sense of sin, shame, or guilt due to sexual immorality dominates this article. The online activities of teenage girls leave nothing to be secret about, according to this review.

Now, here is the irony. Inside the church, people cover up secrets that need to be confessed in the appropriate way, to the appropriate people, and at the appropriate time. Outside the church, all secrets seem to be out. The secular world is a Kardashian world, which presents the wrong kind of openness. Theirs is an openness that does not recognize sin as sin. Yet inside the church, those who do recognize sin as sin hide it rather than appropriately confess and forsake it.

> *The secular world is a Kardashian world, which presents the wrong kind of openness.*

How many people need healing from past sexual abuse, obsessions, escapades, adulteries, perversions, and lapses? Only God Himself knows. Yet such secret-telling must stay within the boundaries of appropriate Christian confession.

During the great awakening that came out of the remarkable Asbury College Revival in 1970, an incredible 144

---

7 Zoe Heller, "Hot Sex and Young Girls," in The New York Review of Books (August 18, 2016), pp. 22-23. This article reviews two new books on the subject of female teenage sexual activity. These books themselves advocate shameless activity as they report on the inability of such young women to engage in it appropriately.

unbroken hours of revival occurred, centering around the school chapel. The sparks from this revival started flames elsewhere. There was much needed confession but also at the same time harmful confession. One male student stood to confess that he lusted after another female student who was named and present when he confessed. This was uncalled for, unbiblical, and hurtful. Past sexual secrets need to be confessed first to God and then to a limited group of people who will not be hurt by the confession, but who can hear it and be used by God to assure the confessors that they can repent of their sin.

> *Past sexual secrets need to be confessed first to God and then to a limited group of people who will not be hurt by the confession, but who can hear it and be used by God to assure the confessors that they can repent of their sin.*

Gregory A. Boyd, in his pastoral wisdom, has written *Seeing Is Believing: Experience Jesus through Imaginative Prayer.*[8] In this book, Boyd presents an approach to prayer wherein folks imagine Jesus coming to them and healing the deepest hurts of their lives. He presents methods to demonstrate how Jesus can come to us in our

---

8 Gregory A. Boyd, *Seeing Is Believing: Experience Jesus through Imaginative Prayer* (Grand Rapids, MI: Baker Books, 2004).

imagination to show up in our broken situations and put us back together again. Whether or not you agree with his specific approach, something like this needs to happen inwardly and personally as an essential part of any dealings with secrets.

IF A CREDIT CARD BILL COULD TALK

A review of anyone's cash receipts, checks, credit card bills, and PayPal account infallibly reveals their priorities and activities. The businessman who draws three hundred dollars out of a joint checking account to spend it on an escort service, the woman who joins an online forum dedicated to married women's affairs, and a lonely old man who uses his social security check to gamble online all have secrets revealed by their use of money.

When you dig beneath most problems, at some point you can "follow the money,"

Sometimes such individuals' secrets are merely humorous. A wealthy doctor hides his dog account from his wife. That dog account includes tuition to a boarding school dog college where the dog learns to point and be a retriever. This secret dog account reveals something less than complete honesty with one's spouse, but it does not rock anyone's world. On the other hand, a manufacturer's rep who falsifies expense reports from trade shows to feed a drug habit has a damaging secret.

A wife suddenly takes half of the money in a joint bank account and transfers it to a secret account inaccessible to her husband. Suddenly bills coming due are not payable, trust is broken, and the marriage is shattered. The husband then shuts down the joint account and places all of his earnings in his own secret account, trusting his wife only enough to give her money for food and medicine. The situation splits the couple, and the marriage becomes unsustainable.

> *Individuals and couples with money deceit need to gather a panel of trusted friends who will hold them accountable while acknowledging their own brokenness.*

All of these represent variations on a theme: money, greed, covetousness, and deceit. When you dig beneath most problems, at some point you can "follow the money," the phrase popularized in the 1976 movie *All the President's Men*. Often, sex problems lead to money problems, or money problems lead to sex problems. And both primarily remain hidden, covert, and unconfessed until homes are blown apart and marriages dissolved.

Individuals and couples with money deceit need to gather a panel of trusted friends who will hold them accountable while acknowledging their own brokenness (Galatians 6:1). Everything needs to be put on the table in a spirit of grace and forgiveness. A line needs to be drawn on the calendar. All secrets before that line are told, and total commitment to honesty on tomorrow's side of that line needs to be kept.

THE POWER PLAY

Still other secrets have to do with power. In every marriage, home, office, school, and church, there are always power plays underway. We don't usually label them by that phrase, but they go on ceaselessly. One co-worker corners a project and drives it unilaterally to make sure no one else gets any credit. A teacher uses inside knowledge to get a position at the school that others deserved much more. A wife knows her husband faked his academic credentials and claimed a degree that got him his current job even though he never finished school. In every argument, she holds that secret over his head and threatens to reveal it to his employer. A sub-contractor leverages his secret knowledge that a general contractor got a kickback on a county project to force the contractor to give him more work. The varieties

These power plays work in the short run. But in the long run, power secrets destroy businesses, marriages, and churches.

are endless, but the theme is always the same: one person uses the power of a secret to control, intimidate, or use another person. It is the endless power game.

These games go on at every level. Franz Joseph, the emperor of the Hapsburg Austrian Empire for sixty-eight years, married a beautiful country girl named Elizabeth when she was fifteen years of age. She had no power and was married to the last divine right emperor of that

To live a whole life, it is always better to be on board, collaborative, and helpful.

regime. Her biography involves a long story of gaining power and using it against her husband. It is an intriguing story of how powerless people can use secrets to get power.

These power plays work in the short run. But in the long run, power secrets destroy businesses, marriages, and churches. Sooner or later the secret comes out, the conversations erupt in bitterness, and relationships are broken. To live a whole life, it is always better to be on board, collaborative, and helpful. One husband frustrated in a marriage ruined by various power plays decided to end the deadlock by asking his wife every morning, "What can I do for you, honey?" She was so stunned by his new attitude that first morning, she cynically said, "Clean the kitchen." He did it. The next morning he asked the same thing, and she snarled, "Clean the garage." Despite days of being on the receiving end of these snide, snarky remarks, he continued to do what she asked. Finally, one morning she totally broke down and confessed her role in their marital discord. He had found a way to stop the power plays, break the log jam, and help heal the marriage.

WHEN THE TIDE GOES OUT

Warren Buffet, the zillionaire investor, has a lot of down-home sayings. One of them has to do with economic downturns and what they reveal about a company's solvency: "When the tide goes out, you find out who really has on a swimsuit." That is to say, some men in the water may act like they have on swim trunks when the tide is high. But when it goes out, it exposes those who do not have on a suit. That vivid statement relates to life's secrets about sex, money, and power. Sooner or later, the tide goes out in life and what we have been hiding underwater is seen for what it is.

Thus, we all better have on a swimsuit.

SEARCHING THROUGH OUR SECRETS

1. When have you seen anyone receive a short-term gain from keeping secrets? How long did that last?

2. What is the principal difference between family secrets and other kinds of secrets?

3. Have you considered biblical families remote and unlike contemporary families, or do you see in those ancient families patterns reflected in your own family?

4. Do you actually believe all secrets will someday be outed?

5. What should you tell someone right now to make a secret lose its power?

"Silence is a lie that screams at the light."

-Sharon L. Alder

Chapter 11

CAMOUFLAGE

Since 1991 I have been friends with the *Duck Dynasty* family, the Robertson's. Even folks who have never seen a duck in the wild, much less shot one, know who they are. Part of their logo and fame involves camouflage. Whether they're wearables, trucks, or "all things camo", camouflage is part of their famous brand. Yet this is sheer irony. The Robertson's are beloved because personally they are anything but camouflaged. Their openness about their family, relationships, beliefs, and lifestyle have endeared them to people who live in high-rises in New York City and apartments in Los Angeles. They wear camo for the less important matter of sending ducks into the life beyond, but they wear no camo when it comes to their own lives. Their transparency is evident.

When David had arranged the execution of Uriah to cover up the pregnancy of the faithful soldier's wife, Bathsheba, he wore spiritual camo. He tried to act as if nothing had happened. Finally, he had to confess that his sin has made him sick:

> *When I kept silence, my bones grew old*
> *Through my groaning all the day long*
> *For day and night your hand was heavy upon me;*
> *My vitality was turned into the drought of summer.*
> *I acknowledged my sin to You,*
> *And my iniquity I have not hidden.*
> *I said, "I will confess my transgression to the Lord,"*
> *And You forgave the iniquity of my sin.*
>
> (PSALM 32:3-5)

David decided to stop wearing camo, and he became whole again. Likewise for us, it is time to take off the camo.

What helps in the natural world can hurt in the spiritual world. God's creative activity in nature is never more astonishing than the camouflage He designed for the animal world. An owl so blends in with a tree trunk that you cannot see the owl. A frog can do the same thing on another tree. An insect looks so much like a stick, it is safe from predators. Camouflage ensures the survival of animal species.

Humans wear camo for hobbies and survival. The wild-turkey hunter wraps his shotgun in camo, covers his body, hands, and face with camo, sits behind a camo net, and tries to hide from the turkey that has the eyes of an eagle when confronted by a hunter. Sitting in the heat with ants literally in your pants, breathless, windless, and motionless, you may still be seen by the vigilant turkey. But that matters little because you are only hunting a turkey. On the other hand, military camo is a matter of life and death. The patterns, shades, and deployment of such camo is a serious matter of personal survival.

Would it surprise you to know that there is also spiritual camo? We can become experts at hiding ourselves from transparency, authenticity, and genuineness. We may hide behind the camo of role expectation, family reputation, spiritual imitation, and defensive reactions, just to name a few.

> *It is of great significance that the first couple, Adam and Eve, reacted to their sin of disobedience by hiding.*

It is of great significance that the first couple, Adam and Eve, reacted to their sin of disobedience by hiding. Since they apparently had no other camo, they tried to blend in behind some vine or tree in the garden. It would have worked if they were hiding from another human being, yet they were trying to hide from God Himself. He had no trouble detecting their camo and called them out immediately.

This is the oldest story in the world of hiding a secret—literally, a secret at the very beginning. We can learn something about all secrets by looking at this original secret.

First, it was a sinful secret in spite of the goodness of God.

The generosity of God is abundant in Genesis 1-2. He puts the first pair in a garden where they can have everything except one thing. He gave them dominion over everything in the garden. They even get to name the animals! While nothing else God created speaks, they have the gift of speech. They walk with God Himself. How good God was to them! Yet in the face of all that, they kept their secret of disobedience from God.

> *All of our secrets always counter the face of God's goodness. God provides for us all that we need, but we devise ways to steal more.*

All of our secrets always counter the face of God's goodness. God provides for us all that we need, but we devise ways to steal more. God gives us companions in life, but we want someone else. God gives us a day of rest, but we want to use it for our own workaholic agenda. And still we think we can keep this a secret from God.

Our secrets also defy the face of God's generosity. He is a God who gives as readily as a rose gives fragrance or the sun gives light because it is His very nature to do so. He gave that first couple a beautiful garden with watering rivers on a perfect earth and dominion over it all. He gave them to one another, the perfect zenith of His creation. He gave them the great and fulfilling joy of sex with one another so they could be fruitful and enjoy one another. He gave them everything except one thing, the tree of the knowledge of good and evil. And yet that was not enough. Their secret rested in their distrust of the generosity of God.

In Honduras, Compassion International serves people who live on less than two dollars a day. They live in huts made of found plastic and wood with dirt floors next to a polluted river. They do not have running water or electricity. They do not know where their next meal is coming from, yet many of them are grateful for what they

> *How many of us deceive ourselves by thinking that we can hide from God Himself?*

do have. How shameful it is for anyone reading this page to compare our abundant lives with theirs. Yet we keep secrets from God in the face of His generosity.

Although one of them initiated the secret, they were both keepers of the secret. (It is very rare, especially in a family, that only one person keeps a secret. Family members almost always talk; they cannot help it. Secrets will come out.) Adam and Eve hid their secret together, but their shame soon spoiled their relationship. When God confronted them, Adam blamed Eve and Eve blamed the snake. They both must have blamed the apple on the tree. The problem, however, was not the apple on the tree but the pair on the ground. Secrets spoil relationships and create a new level of tension and suspicion.

All of this led them to hide unsuccessfully. How many of

us deceive ourselves by thinking that we can hide from God Himself? The psalmist stated this in some of the most beautiful and memorable words in the Scriptures:

Where can I go from Your Spirit?
Or where can I flee from Your presence?
If I ascend into heaven, you are there.
If I make my bed in hell, behold You are there.
If I take the wings of the morning and dwell
in the uttermost parts of the sea,
Even there Your hand shall lead me,
And your right hand shall hold me.

(PSALM 139:7-10)

How do you hide from Someone who is at the same time higher and lower than you can ascend or descend? How can you hide from One who speeds across the sky faster than the rays of the rising sun? Our first misstep is deluding ourselves that our secret is hidden from God Himself. When we hide from God, we are actually hiding from ourselves. So, the first step out of secrecy is to out the secret with God.

Adam and Eve lived in fear until God took the initiative and found them. Like all carriers of secrets, Adam's first defense was to blame God for giving him the woman. It is as if Adam said to God Himself, "If you had not given me the apple-eating woman, I would not be in this pickle." This is almost always the defensive reaction of those who keep secrets.

This blame game can take bizarre shapes. My alma mater, Baylor University, has a strict student policy in comparison with state universities. It can, will, and must because it is a private Christian university. Yet some students in various kinds of trouble have blamed the policies of the university for their moral failures or related secrets. Even the secular press has blamed the university. One newspaper made the school responsible for unreported rapes because the victims were too ashamed to tell their parents that secret. This is blame-placing in the extreme.

> *Even when we are innocent, we tend to blame others for us keeping our secrets.*

Regardless of our guiltless status, our own innocence, and our own righteousness, some of us keep secrets and blame others when we would not tell the secret. Any young woman who is the victim of rape is not guilty. Rape is a terrible crime. In every scenario of the rape of a woman, it is not her fault. Yet at the same time, she cannot blame the university that its strictness made her unwilling to tell her parents. Even when we are innocent, we tend to blame others for us keeping our secrets. Yet there comes a moment of decision when we must tell the secret.

In His great mercy, God does not leave us with our secrets. If I were God, I would have left Adam and Eve to stay in their own hiding place. But God is God and not a man. The God of all cosmic creation showed up in the garden of a tiny planet in His vast cosmos and sought out the first couple to lance the boil of their infected secret.

The Witness Protection Program began in 1970 with the intent of hiding those who turned state's evidence against colleagues in crime or who otherwise would be at risk for reprisal and revenge. To this point, something like eighty-five hundred persons have been given new IDs, new locations, and new starts to hide them from those against whom they testified. Along with them, ninety-five hundred family members have also gone into hiding. Some 95 percent of those in the program were criminals themselves. The government hides criminals who have turned against other criminals.

> *God does not sponsor "witness protection" but a "heavenly truth-in-living" program.*

Yet the evidence is that for a significant number of them, this hidden life is not what it is cracked up to be. They are cut off from their family of origin, community, neighborhood, and all the associations that make life what life is. They find out that even federally funded hiding is not a pleasant thing. A significant number of them quit the program, even at their own risk, because they cannot stand the secrecy.

Fortunately, God does not sponsor a witness protection program. He intends for us to come out from hiding and be real with Him, and as much as necessary, be open to significant others who need to know our secret. God does not sponsor "witness protection" but a "heavenly truth-in-living" program. Transparency, authenticity, openness, and candor—speaking the truth in love—mark the will of the Father in our lives.

When Adam and Eve owned who they were to disown what they had become, God acted in grace by making coverings for them. That metaphor in Genesis can mean any number of things. Surely it foretells the coming of a Savior whose shed blood covers us with God's saving mercy. But it suggests other things as well. No covering we can make is adequate in comparison with the

No covering we can make is adequate in comparison with the gracious covering God makes.

gracious covering God makes. God did not continue forever to blame them, confront them, or badger them with their sin and failure. Having confronted them, He covered them. That is, He did not wish to expose them to further shame and self-loathing.

A friend was once confronted by a wise nationally known pastor for a failure in his life. That pastor asked a remarkable question in their private conversation: "What is the worst thing I can know about you?" My friend confessed his failure in the face of that gentle but provocative question. The renowned pastor then became the greatest sponsor and largest promoter of my friend. He uncovered but then he covered.

God is that kind of God when it comes to our secrets. The story is as old as Eden itself. He will not let us hide. His grace finds us, His mercy forgives us, and then His love covers us.

WHERE ARE YOU HIDING?

We do not so much read the Bible as the Bible reads us. The text is in the congregation and the congregation is in the text. Are you hiding in plain sight? When you think you are hiding from God, that is always the case. No tree in the garden that God made could hide persons from Him. Do you now feel in the quiet of night that Someone knows your secret? Do you not sense that there is One who, even though unseen, knows you through and through? Most thoughtful human creatures have that sense. They know there is Someone from whom they are really not hiding. He is always there, and you cannot escape His loving and ever-present gaze. There is no tree that can hide you from Him.

Yet ironically, He sent His Son to another tree, a tree on Calvary. There He could not hide. In open nakedness and shame, He bled and died, exposed for all the world to see in time and space. He bowed under a tree in Gethsemane and embraced the tree on Calvary so you and I can come from behind all the trees where we hide in the garden that is His anyway. It is time to step out from behind the tree where you are hiding and flee to the tree that makes you free.

SEARCHING THROUGH OUR SECRETS

1. We don't have trouble encouraging others to 'unload their secrets', but why do we tend to hide our secrets?

2. Are there any secrets that are best left with God and God alone?

3. Do you have a friend, counselor, or spiritual confidant that you can share any camouflaged secret with?

4. Do you have a 'trash collector' type of friend where your 'trash' is 'safe' with them?

NO MORE
SECRETS

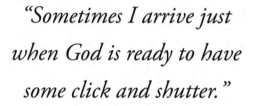

*"Sometimes I arrive just
when God is ready to have
some click and shutter."*

-ANSEL ADAMS

CHAPTER TWELVE

THE GENTLE HANDLER OF SECRETS

For Christians the singular question is straightforward: What does Jesus do about our secrets? Does He expose them without mercy? Does He avoid them to make us comfortable? Does He help us rationalize them to excuse them? Is He indifferent? John 4 reveals comprehensively how Jesus deals with secrets. It tells you how He prearranges situations to deal with your secrets privately, how He goes about revealing your secrets to you, how He gently guides you to see the way out of your secrets, and how He can use you once He has confronted your secrets.

AN ARRANGED ENCOUNTER

In Jesus' time Jews walked around Samaria rather than through it. They thought they would get some kind of spiritual cooties if they walked through the country between Galilee and Judea. To the surprise of His disciples, Jesus insisted on walking

139

through Samaria. This set the table for what He intended to do. A beginning chess player can think only three moves ahead. A chess master can think thirty moves ahead—all the way to checkmate. How many moves ahead can the Son of

He prearranged the timing to guarantee privacy and confidentiality in discussing her secrets.

God think? As many as He needs. The foreknowledge of Jesus enabled Him to know He would encounter a woman with a bag full of secrets at a famous well in Samaria.

The normal time for drawing water from a well was early morning because of the blazing heat of that place. Before the superheated desert air could roast them, the young women of the village gathered at first light to draw water. It was a time of chatter, gossip, plans, and laughter. One woman did not go at that time because the others did not want her there. She had slept with some of their husbands. She was a notorious lecher who voraciously ran through one man after another. She was a gold digger and user, a love-them-and-leave-them machine. She knew she would kill the early morning party, so she came at midday even though the sun scorched her because the well was lonely and quiet.

Jesus intended to meet her at that isolated place and lonely moment. The purpose for His prearrangement was privacy. He sent His own disciples away to find something to eat while He sat with weariness on the paved stone curve of the well. He prearranged the timing to guarantee privacy and confidentiality in discussing her secrets.

Some misguided spiritual leaders and counselors demand that secrets be handled in a way that most humiliates and belittles the ones with the secrets. Shaming, public revelations, forced confessions, coerced disclosures, and displayed testimonies are their bag of tricks. Yet Jesus never dealt with anyone that way. You see it most vividly here in John 4, as well as John 8, where Jesus spoke with a woman caught in the very act of adultery.

Whatever your secrets may be, Jesus will deal with them gently. He saved His harshness for the Pharisees, who considered themselves better than everyone else and pretended to have no secrets.

For those of you caught in the web of secrets and trapped in the

Satan wants to accuse, humiliate, depress, and expose. But Jesus wants you to confront your secret and then hand it to Him.

minefield of your own self-destruction, Jesus acts with gentleness and tact. That is, you can trust Jesus with your secrets. As noted in the previous chapter, a friend once needed to be relieved of a deep secret. A wise pastor asked him, "What is the worst thing I can know about you?" It was a masterpiece of indirection. When my friend confessed that secret, the pastor received the answer with grace. He then expressed his trust in my friend, the secret keeper, and his intention to use the relieved confessor for Christian service in the future. Jesus is just like that. Satan wants to accuse, humiliate, depress, and expose. But Jesus wants you to confront your secret and then hand it to Him.

Have you ever prayed an imaginative prayer? Imagine Jesus holding a beautiful basket, the kind of basket woven by the Son of God. It is wide open, receptive, and inviting. Can you imagine placing your secret in Jesus' basket? You look Him straight in His glorious and compassionate eyes and place your secret in His basket. It is gone. He will never take it out, and no one else can get to it. You can indeed put your secret into His basket.

You can indeed put your secret into His basket.

The United States has great amounts of leftover nuclear waste from power plants. It is no longer potent enough to run power plants, but it is still so radioactive it can kill people for thousands of years. What can you do with that stuff? You have to bury it deeply. Yet that presents the problem that thousands of years from now, someone will accidentally dig it up. The federal government needed to make signs that would last for ages. But what if, ten thousand years from now, no one remembers any of today's languages? The government has worked on signs that indicate "No Digging Here" that would communicate to any people at any time. In the same way, God already has His own sign that means "No Digging."

LOWER AND HIGHER MEANINGS: AN ADVENTURE IN MISSING THE POINT

This woman misunderstood Jesus. He was speaking of a higher, holier, and heavier truth that meant He satisfies our deepest inner needs. Yet she was thinking entirely on a lower, lesser, and lighter level about physical water. She wanted to get into an argument about drawing water from the physical well. Jesus used that metaphor to point to a higher truth: He meets the deepest thirsts of our life for spiritual meaning.

Most of our secrets have to do with the use of sex, money, or power to fulfill the deepest needs of our lives.

Most of our secrets have to do with the use of sex, money, or power to fulfill the deepest needs of our lives. This woman had certainly used sex until sex had used her up. Her entire life had been dominated by sex to the point that she was defined by sex. She had bedded five men and was with yet still another. She was a relationship junkie.

How many folks are like that today? They are always looking for Mr. Right but end up always finding Mr. Half-Right. A series of those encounters leaves one with bitter regret and deep secrets. Such people look at the next relationship as if it were a new box filled with goodies. What they do not know is how much YOU have to put into the box for a relationship to work. The woman at the well had seen six men as six new boxes filled with all kinds of bright and shiny things. Then came the inevitable letdown: the box was empty.

Such searches for meaning in a physical relationship always lead to more emptiness. Those whose lives are given to chasing sex are never satisfied. It is like drinking salt water when you are adrift at sea; the more you drink, the thirstier it makes you. Those who work in retirement centers observe older folks in their eighties. They tell us the most active rooms in the retirement center are those set aside for sex between consenting ancient people! They have to keep wandering old men with dementia from climbing into bed with old women. Such is the endless power of lust that drives the search for meaning in life.

Yet many of our deepest secrets have to do with covering up illicit acts of sex. Politicians demonstrate the lengths to which they, as people of power, will go to cover up past sinful sex acts. This woman had a multitude of sex secrets, yet consider how gently Jesus dealt with her.

A SIGNIFICANT INDIRECTION

Jesus did not open the conversation with a confrontational question such as, "How does it feel to be a five-time loser?" He started as indirectly and evocatively as possible by asking the woman for a drink of well water. Nothing could have been gentler. In fact, it was so gentle that it startled her because Jews and Samaritans did not drink from the same gourds.

It was an extreme case of the old-fashioned cooties. Do you remember the cooties from elementary school? The Jews practiced avoiding spiritual cooties. They acted as if they would get a spiritual infection if they touched anything a Samaritan touched. Jesus, however, was different. He practiced a sort of reverse cooties. He was more contagious than anything He touched. Before He left the well, He would infect this poor woman with His own goodness. She came with her need, and He gave to her from His own abundance. She came with a water pot, but she abandoned it because she was filled with something better. All of this was part of the gentle, indirect approach of Jesus toward sinners like her.

> *They acted as if they would get a spiritual infection if they touched anything a Samaritan touched.*

It is interesting to contrast this gentleness with His harsh treatment of the Pharisees. He was direct and confrontational with those who claimed to have no secrets. He was relentless in His condemnation of those who refused to acknowledge their own brokenness. He had mercy and grace for those willing to confront their secrets, but royal, lordly rejection for those who claimed to have none. Your secrets are safe with Jesus, but you are not safe with Him if you claim to have no secrets. He was relentless in His judgment of those who claimed to be above having any secrets.

LET'S TALK ABOUT RELIGION RATHER THAN OUR SECRETS

We are so resistant to opening up about our secrets that we would rather do anything else. This woman suddenly started a theological argument about the best place to go to church. The Samaritans had their own temple that competed with the temple in Jerusalem. She wanted to discuss advanced ecclesiology: where you should go to church. So deep is her desire to avoid discussing her secrets that this woman sleeping with her sixth man suddenly turns into a theologian to avoid the conversation!

Yet Jesus does not hammer her with a theological argument. Rather, He gives to this woman one of the most precious truths about the worship of God: "God is Spirit, and those who worship Him must worship in spirit and truth" (v. 24). He cuts to the chase. What this woman needs is not a discussion about which temple to attend. Instead, she needs reality. Jesus may have been the first to say, "Accept no substitutes."

A friend of a friend of mine was visiting the exhibit of First Lady inaugural gowns at the Smithsonian. He was viewing the golden gown worn by Lady Bird Johnson on a mannequin. Sensing someone standing by him, he turned and it was Lady Bird herself. He was looking at the very lady who had worn the gown to the inaugural ball, and that stunned him to silence. Then a strange thing happened. A photographer gruffly asked him and Lady Bird to move out of the way so he could take a picture of the gown on the dummy. Lady Bird quietly left without saying a word. The man with the camera could have captured a photo of a living First Lady, but he settled for a picture of a dummy with a gown on. He missed the real thing while taking a shot of a dummy!

Everybody wants relief from their secrets, and Christ is the One who can bear the secrets of all.

In the same way, this Samaritan woman was standing in front of reality. But she did not even know it until Jesus revealed His true identity to her.

LEAVING WHAT YOU CAME WITH

When Jesus kindly revealed to this woman that He is the Messiah, she left her water pot at the well (v. 28). When she met Jesus, she left the thing she brought with her. She ran back into the town and told the men, likely many she had slept with, that she had found someone who told her all of her secrets. She wondered out loud if this is the Christ. They all left town and ran to the well with her. Indeed, everybody wants relief from their secrets, and Christ is the One who can bear the secrets of all.

My favorite story by Ernest Hemingway is entitled "The Capital of the World." It is about a boy named Paco (a common name in Spain) who had run away because of a disagreement with his father.

No one could really say why he ran away. Or perhaps he didn't, but he was kicked out of the house by his father for something foolish that he said or did. Either way, Paco found himself wandering the streets of Madrid, Spain, with hopes of entering into a profession that would most likely get him killed—bullfighting. Those who train under a mentor have a good chance of surviving in this profession, but Paco's memory of his mistakes and guilt over what happened blindly drove him to this one-way street to suicide.

But that was the last thing his father wanted. He tried something desperate, which he desperately hoped would work. There was little to no chance that he would be able to find Paco by wandering the streets of Madrid, so instead he put an advertisement in the local newspaper *El Liberal*. The advertisement read, "Paco, meet me at the Hotel Montana at noon on Tuesday. All is forgiven! Love, Papa."

Paco is such a common name in Spain that when the father went to the Hotel Montana the next day at noon there were eight hundred young men named Paco waiting for their fathers . . . and waiting for the forgiveness they never thought was possible!

In the same way, we are all Paco. All of those men following that wayward woman running through the sand in the heat of the noonday were Paco. We all want someone to tell us that our secrets are forgiven.

That is the wonder of the Christian life. They really are forgotten. God can no longer remember our sinful secrets. Once we confess them and try to tell God about them again, He gently says, "What are you talking about? I don't know anything about it." The Father really does forgive.

> *God is the original inventor of the heavenly marker board. Tell Him your secrets, and they are erased forever.*

When I was a little boy, the public schools still used blackboards and chalk. Even when you used an eraser to erase the white chalk, it still left a very faint residue of what had been written. You just could not get rid of it totally. Then came the marker boards of today. You can totally erase anything you put there. God is the original inventor of the heavenly marker board. Tell Him your secrets, and they are erased forever.

One can only wonder what kind of father this woman at the well had. The Bible does not tell us. I can guess that due to her relationships with men, he may not have been an ideal father. Countless men and women have not had good fathers. Martin Luther's father was so terrible that Luther had a hard time praying the Lord's Prayer that begins with, "Our Father . . ." Mozart's father exploited his gifted son, so much so that many despise Leopold Mozart for how he used Wolfgang Amadeus. I have a good friend and treasured mentor who told me, "I do not have one good memory of my father." I once asked him, "Have you ever gotten over your father?" His sad response was, "No."

That gives us all the more reason to rejoice that Jesus promised a Father who is always a Father to the fatherless. And He will be our heavenly Father forever.

SEARCHING THROUGH OUR SECRETS

1. How do you use indirection when helping hurting or failing people? Do you have a method of coming at a problem "on the slant" rather than smash-mouth directness and perpetual bluntness?

2. Can you remember a time when someone helped you by indirect conversation rather than confrontation? How did it feel?

3. What role does timing play in the way you deal with other people? Do you recognize there is a time to speak and a time to refrain from speaking?

4. Can you remember a troubled time when you said something, and the moment after you said it you knew you should not have done so?

5. What was another time Jesus used indirectness in His approach to someone in need? Consider John 3 and His approach to Nicodemus or John 21 and His restoration of Peter. In what ways was Jesus indirect?

"*Many realities are hidden behind a wall of perception.*"

-TOBA BETA

CHAPTER 13

RESURRECTING SECRETS: GETTING PAST THE STINK

Some folks bury their dead in crypts. A crypt is usually a small space in a mausoleum, where they place a casket above ground. Mausoleums are filled with ugly boxes molded out of rough, unfinished concrete. In a stark and bizarre contrast with that, the fronts of the boxes are covered with beautiful marble. When you enter a mausoleum, it appears to be a beautiful place. Stained glass windows, gentle mists of perfume, soft music, gilded letters with the deceased names, and floral tributes make the place look gorgeous.

The truth, however, is very different. Those thin marble facades hide a gruesome truth: thousands of folks are decaying, decomposing, and deteriorating within the boxes.

The English adjective "cryptic," derived from the very place described, is another word for anything that is hidden or secretive. A cryptic situation is one in which something has been hidden and it would not smell very good if it all came out.

Jesus encountered a situation like that. His close friend Lazarus had died. Lazarus' two sisters, Mary and Martha, sent for Jesus to tell him that His friend was sick. While Jesus waited two days to go to his friends' house, Lazarus died in the meantime. One of the most vivid and moving stories in the New Testament is the account of Jesus' encounter with Lazarus' surviving sisters. Martha remonstrates and Mary pouts. Jesus uses the occasion to announce one of His great I AM sayings: "I am the resurrection and the life" (John 11:25).

> *The family had placed a stone in front of the crypt to hide the obvious.*

An edgy scene follows. Jesus goes out to the tomb of his friend. (The crypt of Lazarus was carved into the rocky hillside of Bethany. The family had placed a stone in front of the crypt to hide the obvious.) Jesus ordered them to move the stone. I like the old King James Version: "Surely he stinketh." Moving the stone would foul the air of that hot climate with the stench of death itself. Yet without hesitation Jesus insisted they move the stone.

The sequel has been narrated, portrayed, and presented in epic movies. Lazarus walks out bound in the grave clothes of that day, wrapped round and round with linen strips intermingled with spices. Jesus commands them to unwrap him and let him go. Later they all have dinner at the Bethany home. Lazarus, however, never says a thing.

BURIED SECRETS

Everyone I know has buried some secrets somewhere. They may be locked up in papers in a safety deposit box. They could be in a shoebox in the attic—old letters that would embarrass us if they were found and read. Some secrets are buried in the records of cell phone calls, text messages, or websites visited in the middle of the night.

> *Secrets buried in the crypt of memory tend to resurrect in the presence of eternity and judgment.*

Sometimes those secrets tell themselves. A couple is so close they eat food from the same take-out box, finish one another's sentences, enjoy the same books and movies, and practically share the same life every day. Then one night a text message is discovered, and the innocent spouse finds there is a third spoke in their wheel. An unwanted stinking secret comes out. There is someone else who brings disharmony into their otherwise untroubled world.

Folks bury things for two reasons. First, they bury valuable stuff, and they do not want it to be stolen. On the other hand, they also may bury stuff that is embarrassing, and they do not want it to be found. In the tragicomic movie, *A Family Thing*, Earl Pilcher, Jr.'s (Robert Duvall) mother is dying. He finds out from a letter written by her that his aging, demented father (James N. Harrell) had slept with a black woman (Patrice

Pitman Quinn) in the Jim Crow South and Duvall has a black half-brother, Ray Murdock (James Earl Jones), in Chicago. His dying mother wants Earl to know his unknown brother. Earl drives to Chicago, and the encounter between him and Ray is both tragic and comic as the family secret comes out. The prejudiced Southerner and his Chicago half-sibling argue, fight, and insult, but finally reconcile. The movie ends with their unforgettable visit to an overgrown cemetery, where they hug each other by a long abandoned black church. They both look at the grave where Ray's mother is buried. The revealing of the secret hurt, but it ended up creating a new, redemptive, and loving relationship.

Not everyone's buried secret results in such drama. People do, however, tend to tell secrets at the end of life, and you might want to get ready for it. Secrets buried in the crypt of memory tend to resurrect in the presence of eternity and judgment. Buried stuff can come to life.

MOVE THE STONE AND LET THE ROT OUT

Jesus' command to move the stone before there could be a resurrection is a striking statement. Jesus is about to raise a man from the dead who has been in the tomb for four days. The Jews believed that the spirit hung around the grave, but after four days it was gone. The man was deader than dead. Did you ever wonder why Jesus told the bystanders to move the stone? Jesus was about to pull off the biggest miracle in history, raising a dead man after four days. Jesus could have pointed to the stone with His finger like a laser and vaporized it, or He could have put the stone into orbit. Jesus could even have made the stone roll down the hill all the way to the Jordan River miles away. But Jesus told them to do what they could do.

Without being gross or offensive, this was a "stinking" situation. In the Holy Land, then and now, burial usually occurs the same day. The blazing sun hastens the decomposition processes, so burial must be soon. Opening a tomb four days after the burial of a corpse would unleash all the unpleasantness associated with this. Those who moved the stone

> *We cannot tell exactly what happened in this exact situation, but they had to risk the stink to see the resurrection.*

feared exposure to just such a thing. We cannot tell exactly what happened in this exact situation, but they had to risk the stink to see the resurrection. Perhaps the tomb of Lazarus was actually like the martyrdom of Polycarp, the aged Christian. When he was burned at the stake, a sweet perfume filled the air.

The important thing to note is this: it took a community to remove the shroud of secrecy and loose Lazarus to enjoy the new life set before him. The bystanders gathered around him, and together they stripped off the grave clothes. This is how church should be, but how church seldom is. We seem shocked senseless to uncover someone's secret. An unfaithful spouse, a cheating businessperson, a hidden hatred, or a deep bitterness often leaves church folks so paralyzed that we are unable to gather around and remove the grave clothes. We pretend we are in our Sunday finest when instead we are all coming out of our own tombs. What I know about prominent persons' secrets and hurts could fill this book, and you would be shocked speechless. Yet the church should be the place where we help one another remove the grave clothes. Instead, we act as if we are all wearing new Armani suits while, in fact, we are in shrouds.

> *When we help people confess their secrets, we may encounter the initial unpleasantness that goes with such situations.*

When we help people confess their secrets, we may encounter the initial unpleasantness that goes with such situations. The embarrassment, anger, pain, depression, and despair that comes out when secrets are revealed at first poisons the atmosphere. But then, resurrection happens.

RESURRECTION CHANGES THE ATMOSPHERE

Whatever the stench might have been, it was quickly forgotten when Lazarus walked out of the tomb. We should note that there was a process. Lazarus was bound up in grave clothes. Jesus asked those around to do what they could do to participate. With trembling hands and bated breath, the bystanders loosed him and let him go. Perhaps his first few steps were tentative, but one can imagine the joy of his reunion with Mary and Martha, not to mention his gratitude to Jesus. On the other side of the stench was joy, renewal, unbelievable relief, and release.

The initial dread and malodorous moment of letting secrets come out of their tombs gives way to a sense of relief, joy, and new beginnings. The boil is lanced, the wound is cleansed, and the brief pain of light striking the eyes coming out of the dark gives way to a new sense of health and insight. There is no freedom like the freedom of coming out of a secretive life.

You too can know the relief that comes from shedding the death rags and grave clothes of secrecy, emerging out of the crypt, and enjoying the rising sun and fresh breeze of another day.

Two United States presidents in my lifetime at first lied to the public about their secretive situations. Nixon refused to confess his involvement in Watergate, and Clinton declined to admit that he was having an affair. (I am using the names of Presidents from both political parties, so don't send me an angry e-mail.) I have to wonder what relief both of them finally felt when they could no longer hide what had happened. Their lives could not go on until the secret was resolved. Nixon was haunted in the

White House halls, and Clinton had to hide from his wife and daughter. Yet, I expect both felt a strange new freedom when the secret was out.

Although your confession may not be so public and dramatic, you too can know the relief that comes from shedding the death rags and grave clothes of secrecy, emerging out of the crypt, and enjoying the rising sun and fresh breeze of another day. God's Spirit/wind blows away the foul odor of secrets and cleanses the air to be as fresh as a morning walk on a beach by an azure sea, where every wind is fresh and every breath is easy.

SEARCHING THROUGH OUR SECRETS

1. Have you ever helped someone come out of secrecy and into open confession? How did you feel?
2. What has the Holy Spirit revealed to you that is buried in your own heart that needs to come out?
3. Once God has forgiven you, do not put your secret back into the crypt. Do you truly accept the forgiveness of God as a real event? You do not have to bury it and dig it up repeatedly. Don't act like Dracula.
4. Do you act with grace towards people whom you know are carrying secrets? They are under a

heavy burden and need graciousness rather than back-stabbing gossip. When did Jesus ever gossip about anyone?

5. Have you ever avoided someone because they know what is buried in your own life? How did that feel?

"*Detachment means letting go,
and nonattachment
simply means letting be.*"

—STEPHEN LEVINE

CHAPTER 14

ATTACHMENT
AND DETACHMENT:
THE END OF SECRETS

S ecrets are indeed like radioactivity: They can either bless
or blast. When radioactivity is used in x-rays or for fight-
ing disease, it helps to heal. Yet in those same rooms where
people are healed, there are bright-red signs on the doors
warning us that too much radioactivity can take life rather
than give it. Likewise, there is a fine balance between revealing too little and too much. I call that "the end of secrets."
The word "end" can have two meanings. On the one hand,
it can note the conclusion of something. Yet, yours truly also
learned at seminary that the "end" of something may also
indicate its purpose, or its intention. One old buddy of mine
said, "What end do you have in mind?" He meant, "What is
your purpose?"

A HEALTHY BALANCE

Healthy relationships consist of both holding on and letting go. Unhealthy attachment to someone—and their secrets—means a total involvement with that person in their emotional, spiritual, and physical energy. Listening to secrets and empathizing about them, along with helping people through secrets, drains you if you do it right. Even Jesus knew when someone had drawn the energy of healing out of Him (Mark 5:30).

If you hold the bird too loosely, it may fall out and injure itself. But if you hold the bird too tightly, you can suffocate the bird.

Trying to meet every need of another person sets you up for inevitable failure. There is only One—God Himself—who is capable of meeting all the needs of all the people. In addition, when you allow someone to sap you of all spiritual energy and drain you of all mental power and emotional reserves, you not only fail to help them but you put yourself at risk.

The pastor of a close friend's home church lived in a neighborhood where a murder had taken place. He knew the persons involved, so he became obsessed with solving the crime. I guess he thought he was Rev. Columbo, with apologies to Peter Falk. (If you are too young to remember that show, it is now on the Hallmark channel.) He got so involved with such empathy and concern about the situation, he eventually lost his ministry, even though he was a good pastor and a beloved leader. Some tried to dissuade him from his attachment but failed. That is an extreme case, yet it underscores the downside of too much attachment to secrets.

The late Dutch theologian Henri Nouwen compared attachment/detachment with holding a baby bird. If you hold the bird too loosely, it may fall out and injure

When it comes to secrets, there comes a time when you must detach.

itself. But if you hold the bird too tightly, you can suffocate the bird. There is a sensitive, perceptive amount of holding on that gives safety and freedom. We see the same phenomenon in "helicopter parents," who hover over their children with such vigilance that both the kids and the parents are lost when Mom and Dad finally must let go.

Even universities are experiencing first hand those parents who cannot let go. A professor told me about a parent who called him and asked the first day of class at a major university, "Where is *our* syllabus?" The parent was referring to a college freshman (her child) and the syllabus for the class. The professor had to remind the mother that the syllabus was not theirs together. Another parent tried to rent a dorm room to live in the same residence hall with his child. This is the outcome of suffocating attention that hurts both the parent and child.

When it comes to secrets, there comes a time when you must detach. The strongest glue known to humans is a polyurethane compound that sticks beyond imagination. You can chain two cars together with it and it will not come loose. Knowing some secrets can be like that. They adhere to you, and you just cannot get loose. That is the time to detach and let the person who told you their secret find their way by the grace of God. Even the Samaritan who helped the man in the ditch in Jesus' famous parable gave the innkeeper some money, wished everyone the best, and moved on with his life (Luke 10:35).

TOO MUCH WORRY OVER SOMEONE ELSE'S SECRET

Simon Wiesenthal wrote a famous book entitled *The Sunflower*.[9] He recalled an astonishing event when he was detained in a concentration camp at Lemberg. With other Jews, he was sent out to do awful work. One day the Nazis marched him to a hospital where he disposed of filth. A nurse took him into a hospital room and left him there. In the room was Karl, a twenty-two-year-old dying Nazi who confessed a sickening secret to Simon. He was an SS man who had forced three hundred Jewish women and children into a building, soaked it with gas, set it on fire, and burned them to death. He shot anyone who tried to run out. Now Karl was dying of wounds and held Simon's hand with a death grip. He wanted Simon,

---

9 Simon Wiesenthal, *The Sunflower* (New York: Schocken Books), 1998.

as a Jew, to forgive him for what Karl had done to other Jews. Simon refused to do so because he did not think it was his place to forgive someone who had wronged helpless men and women. He walked out without granting the forgiveness.

After the war, Simon looked up Karl's mother in Stuttgart. Knowing Karl was dead, she told him what a good boy her son was all his life. Simon faced another dilemma. Should he tell the mother the awful thing her son had done? He decided not to and thus spared her from such grief.

> *God does not intend for us to hear everyone's terrible secrets and so take them into our very souls to the extent that they derail our own lives.*

The famous story recounts Simon's anguish for years after he refused to forgive the Nazi. He went back to the concentration camp and wore his friends out about what he should have done: to forgive or not forgive. Then, he worried about whether he should have told the dead boy's mother the truth. Finally, he asked a symposium of fifty-three future world leaders in various areas what they thought he should have done. Each gave her or his answer at the end of the story. All the answers weighed in on what to do with such a secret. Simon anguished over what he had done with the Nazi soldier's secret and then worried about what he had not told the mother.

This story emphasizes to me that some secrets can literally become too much to bear. God does not intend for us to hear everyone's terrible secrets and so take them into our very souls to the extent that they derail our own lives. Wiesenthal's book is a classic about what to do with a secret and the burden that a secret may become. When you read the book, it makes you weigh what you have done with the secrets that others have told you. Some secrets can indeed just be too much.

PROTECTING THE SECRETS OF OTHERS

You should also understand the Christian responsibility to protect the secrets of others. When a person tells you a secret, it is a sacred trust. That individual had enough faith to hand you their very deepest hurt or failure. That is an act of faith in your willingness to keep a secret a secret. Many of us know about persons who have betrayed the secrets of others or persons who have been betrayed.

If someone has wronged another person, that secret should be between the one harmed and the one who did the harm.

If someone has wronged another person, that secret should be between the one harmed and the one who did the harm. There are too many, even in churches, who delight in gossiping and broadcasting the secret failures of others. But this is never the Christian way. The only time the entire church should know a secret is after an individual has refused an original conversation, another conversation with more folks, and then demonstrates a hardened heart (Matthew 18:15-18). Yet this is an extreme case and is the very last resort. Otherwise, we are supposed to cover one another's secrets with loving care and redemptive intention.

TRUST GOD AND
LET HIM HAVE THE SECRET

A friend of mine who works in hospice care recounted the death of a forty-one-year-old from cancer. He wanted to help the dying man in ways that no human could help. But there comes a time for family, friends, and even chaplains to let go. We came into this world one at a time, and in the words of Dr. Gardner C. Taylor, "We leave one at a time, sometimes through crevices so narrow, we are scarred in the leaving."

Yet God spoke to my friend from the closing words of the 23rd Psalm: "Surely goodness and mercy shall follow me all the days of my life." He reflected that goodness and mercy do not always go before us, but rather we run into things. Life crashes, and the unexpected happens. Goodness and mercy do not even always go alongside us. Some days we feel utterly alone, almost abandoned. Yet goodness and mercy still follow us.

If you are like me, you know you have left some secrets behind in your life that have not caught up with you. When the secrets of others have come out, you have often said, "There, but for the grace of God, go I." You know that God's eternal goodness and unending mercy have kept your own secrets from catching up with you. Like a rear guard in the military, they have protected you from the past and its secrets.

We have talked about who, when, where, why, and how to help others with secrets and deal with our own. But beyond all of that, we can only throw ourselves with reckless abandon on His goodness and mercy. We are headed to that place where we shall know as we are known, all secrets will be over, and there will be no more night and no more tears. There will never again be a secret to hear or tell, other than a thousand secrets we do not know on this side about the power and love of our Lord.

SEARCHING THROUGH THE SECRETS

1. Emotional detachment in psychology can be a positive behavior which allows a person to react calmly to highly emotional circumstances/individuals. Emotional detachment in this sense is a decision to avoid engaging emotional connection, rather than an inability or difficulty in doing so, typically for personal, social, or other reasons. Therefore, what creates the detachment struggle for you? Lies, anger, hurt, pain, or substance abuse?

2. Can you detach and love someone and yourself at the same time?

3. Detachment with love means that I stop depending upon what others do, say or feel to determine my own wellbeing or to make my decisions. In this sense, it can allow people to maintain 'boundaries' related to emotional demands. As such, it is a deliberate mental attitude which avoids engaging the emotions of others. How do you use detachment in your life with certain close family members and friends?

NO MORE SECRETS

"The circumstances we ask God to change are often the circumstances God is using to change us."

-MAX LUCADO

CHAPTER 15

WHEN THE CHARADE IS OVER

As I was nearing completion of this book, God brought me to a complete halt. For several years, my oldest son's life was spinning out of control. I set the manuscript aside and asked, "God, do You really want me to write this? Is there some reason I should not be 'open and honest' about my family?" For several months it sat on my desk, and every day I wondered why "secrets" seemed to haunt me at every turn.

I heard a godly woman say one time her favorite verse began, "And it came to pass . . . ." Then she said, "Isn't that wonderful news?" Think about that! "It came to pass. . . ." In other words, "It's not going to STAY!"

Whatever happens in our lives, or the lives of our family or friends, isn't going to last forever. Whatever we are going through, we can GROW through as well. Healing comes when we are open to the truth and then move forward.

After much prayer and thought, I asked my oldest son if he

would write the closing words of this book. In some ways, it's the culmination of the gravity and weight that secrets can have in someone's life.

He shares the reality and facts of a life where secrets ruled and reigned. Not until the cleansing power of Jesus Christ washes away the stains of hidden sins are we able to live in the light of His redemption.

Have you come to that place in your life? Can you say the following words? "Lord Jesus, I am not going to live this way anymore. Please come into my heart, cleanse and purge my life of the secrets and sins that have robbed me of the abundant life You promise to each of us. I turn my will, my heart, my life, and my secrets over to You today."

This is my prayer for everyone who reads the words of this book. I thank you for allowing me the opportunity to share my life with you. May you find strength to say as I have, "NO MORE SECRETS".

Epilogue

Freedom from Putting on a Charade
By Chad Dennison Swanberg

The first time I heard the words, "No more secrets," they came out of the mouth of my mother. I remember her sitting in the middle of an intervention that my family conducted for me. She stated that she was tired of all the lies, dishonesty, deceit, and deception. And I could understand her disgust; with all the secrecy from her mother, my brother, and I, the masquerade had taken its toll on her. So, when I learned that my father was writing a book with this exact title, I knew that he could share insightfully through his knowledge and life experiences in a way that others might not fully understand.

For me, secrets were the name of the game—the only way to get by. As the oldest son of a preacher, attending Christian schools and colleges, if I fell short in any way of the legalistic rules I believed I was to adhere to, then secrets were a necessity. So, from an early age, I learned how to put on a charade. I learned to be whatever was necessary for me to get by.

At church, I was the cardboard cutout of the perfect Sunday school kid. At school, I was a model student who sat in the front, paid attention, and made good grades. On the field, I was a hard worker and loyal teammate. But on the weekends, I could drink and have a good time like anyone else. And when I picked up a girl for a date and met her parents, I was everyone's All-American. I spent the better part of my life, over three decades, behind a mask of whatever it was that I believed you wanted me to be. So, secrets? Sure, I had a closet full.

Once you have developed a pattern that is so entrenched in dishonesty and lies, you cannot help but continue down that slippery slope. I kept everything from people. I was expected to act a certain way because I was held to a higher standard. I had good jobs, maybe a title or two, credentials, and a place in the community. But it could never be known by anyone what all I was doing. If the truth came out, all would be lost and especially my precious reputation and status eliminated. So, I continued to keep hope that what was "done in the dark would never come to light."

By the time I was an adult, secrecy had become a well-acquired skill. I could convince anyone that I had my life together. I ran for a long time keeping up this appearance, so much so that when I honestly admit my failures and shortcomings today, people are aghast and cannot believe it. Secrets have left me in a place of shame, guilt, remorse, and then starting over. The lie of a life that I have lived has left me picking up the pieces, and trying to begin again. Therefore, I can tell you that secrets make you very sick and can ruin your life.

Secrets have caused me to reach for the bottle, hurt and alienate many of my closest and dearest friends, avoid worshipping in God's house, and waste money I could not afford to throw away foolishly. Secrets have cost me two marriages and landed me in the office of counselors and in rehabilitation on two occasions. Secrets have left me unemployed, scared, and alone. But not only that, secrets have scarred and wounded the people I never wanted to hurt.

My secrets led me to avoid any type of spiritual guidance. At no point would I seek counsel or wisdom from anyone else. With chauvinistic bravado and ego, I chose the role of "hero" and played "God" in my own life. I believed I could handle everything myself. And when things were difficult, I would pull up my big-boy boots, shoulder the load myself, and tell nobody because I was strong enough to handle life on my own.

One of my greatest secrets was my own deception. Although I was very good at deceiving those around me, I was even better at fooling myself. I kept secrets from myself. I avoided responsibility by playing the victim—blaming, justifying, and rationalizing—so that I didn't have to take credit or accountability for my part in my problems. The actions, behaviors, and choices that I made, however, gave me the life that I had. Yet, I was still unwilling to pull the curtain back on that secret. Never would I be willing to confess that I was the reason for my difficulties or responsible for my struggles. I could not admit the secret truth that the answer to my problem stared at me in the mirror every morning. Every secret that I kept had to be protected.

Secrets caused my life to deteriorate from the inside out. Everything was affected because of my secrecy. My marriages fell apart, my work suffered, my personal relationships were strained, my physical health declined, my sobriety crumbled, my spiritual life was bankrupt, and mentally I was haunted with stress and anxiety. Everything I had in the world was spinning out of control and down the drain because I lived in a web of lies.

There is no way to live in the shade of secrecy. For my entire life, I showed you a picture of what I wanted you to believe, or what I thought that you wanted me to be. But this is an effort in futility. The truth will always rear its head—and when it does, there can be destruction of epic proportions.

I have heard it said that if God wants to use a man, He must break him first. Well, in my experience, the breaking comes from the revelation of secrets. The Bible tells us that "the truth will set you free" (John 8:32 ESV). I believe this is accurate. The truth will set you free, but not before it makes you very mad, unhappy, and uncomfortable. The prayer that I always prayed, that what is done in the dark never comes to the light, was not answered. And when I have had to face my secret, that is when the brokenness found root in my callused and hardened heart. But this position was the bottom that I needed to reach before I would begin looking up!

So today, I look back on a life full of secrecy and cringe at its ugliness. I do not like the way that I lived for so long. But the brokenness that I have experienced has changed me. I do not regret the past, nor do I wish to shut the door on it. Today I choose truth over lies and light over darkness. I believe that the difference in individuals is their response to our brokenness. I have a choice: do I ignore it and continue to live in a cave of dark deceit, or do I come out into the light of truth? Do I remain in the dungeon of sickness, or come out into the clean healing air?

I do not know what my contribution to this book is supposed to be; I will leave that in God's hands. But what I do know is that secrets destroy and kill, while truth builds and saves. Secrets destroy relationships and kill your spirit, but truth builds character and saves lives. I also know that there is an incredible freedom when the weight of secrecy is lifted off your shoulders. At times, my life has been a slow trudge through a countless array of hurdles, emotions, issues, and struggles because of my actions, behaviors, and choices. But today I do not have the weight of lies held inside that I am trying to keep from coming into the daylight.

In Alcoholics Anonymous they have "The 12 Steps." In this plan, step five is, "Admit to God, ourselves, and another human being the exact nature of our wrongs." I have taken this step on numerous occasions now that I have stubbornly turned myself over to a life of honesty and openness. What I realized through this process was that my secrets were not earth shattering. The crimes and evils I had committed were not shocking to God. He knew them all, and accepted me and loved me despite myself and my failures. I was not cast out or judged but understood, accepted, and forgiven. Somehow, I believed that I was hiding my sin from God while I was hiding it from everyone else. But He knew all along. He watched and waited, all the while loving me anyway.

Secrets lose their power if they are admitted and shared. Then, suddenly, you can arise and walk again. Today, I am a known and loved child of God. I stumble and falter and fail, but I am forgiven and accepted. I do not have to try to hide my shortcomings or put on a mask of superiority because I know that I am but a beggar amongst beggars, but on occasion I can point someone toward some bread.

"For I am the Lord your God, who takes hold of your right hand and says to you, 'Do not fear . . . . I will help you.'"

ISAIAH 41:13

ABOUT THE AUTHOR

Dennis Swanberg served the local church in pastoral ministry for twenty-three years. Then, in 1995, Dennis took a leap of faith when he stepped down as church pastor and stepped up to the microphone. Soon, the Swan became "America's Minister of Encouragement," a job he takes seriously as he continues to speak to over a hundred and fifty churches and organizations every year. He has hosted two successful TV series, authored nine books, and created over two dozen video projects.

Dennis is a graduate of Baylor University, where he majored in both Greek and Religion (1976). He earned both a Master of Divinity (1980) and a Doctor of Ministry (1986) at Southwestern Seminary, Fort Worth, Texas.

Dennis has been married to Lauree Alica Wilkes of Fort Worth for over thirty-eight years. He also has two grown sons, Chad and Dustin, and a daughter-in-law, Britny. The Swanberg's make their home in Monroe, Louisiana.

If you would like to book Dr. Swanberg to speak for your church, organization, or corporate group, please feel free to contact him by phone at 318-350-9785 or e-mail at swanbergministries@gmail.com. You can also begin the process of booking "the Swan" on his website, www.dennisswanberg.com. There you can find Dr. Swanberg's other books and products as well.

A BRIEF WORD ABOUT
SWANBERG CHRISTIAN MINISTRIES

I sincerely hope that this book, *No More Secrets,* has been a blessing and encouragement to you as you have read through every page. It is our prayer that you find STRENGTH for today, HOPE for tomorrow, and GRACE for every moment.

If the Lord ever directs you to help us at SCM in our "Ministry of Encouragement," just know that we appreciate your consideration. Swanberg Christian Ministries is a non-profit ministry, and we seek to encourage the saints "now that His day is drawing near" (Hebrews 10:25). We also have strong mission ties and partnerships with specific missionary evangelists in Southeast Asia and the Philippines, as well as general missions associated with the International Mission Board.

One of our biggest blessings is continuing to encourage our Unites States military. The Lord has directed our paths to Iraq, Germany, South Korea, and the Middle East. Doors have continued to open at many military bases and hospitals stateside as well. We are honored every opportunity we have to encourage and uplift those who sacrifice so much for our freedom.

Swanberg Christian Ministries
www.dennisswanberg.com
swanbergministries@gmail.com